A basic course in

GRAPHIC DESIGN

It is hoped that this book will serve the purpose of focusing attention on recent developments in a field of visual communication. Richard Taylor places a contemporary graphic design course against an historical background in order to show how modern technology, together with social and industrial pressures, is changing this area of further education. The experimental design course described in this book is the product of the combined thinking of a specialist team of graphic design teachers and practitioners. As the leader of this team, the author not only draws upon twenty years experience in art and design education concerned with graphic design, but also upon a varied experience in freelance industrial applications of graphic communication.

Richard Taylor's experience of operational flying in the Far East and his early training as a flight engineer with such disciplines as controlling and fault-finding (trouble-shooting) in electronic, hydraulic and pneumatic systems, together with his lifelong interest in animal behaviour patterns, may have been amongst the many 'outside' influences that have shaped his views on design education.

Richard Taylor is an Associate of the Royal College of Art and a full member of the Royal West of England Academy of Art. He has practised as a designer in both two- and three-dimensions and has illustrated over twenty books in different media. Since 1965 he has been head of the Graphic Design Department of the West of England College of Art (Bristol Polytechnic). His work has been purchased by the War Artists Committee, the Victoria and Albert Museum and many other public and private collections.

Dedicated to
Jenny Frances and Matthew

A basic course in

GRAPHIC DESIGN

Richard Taylor

Studio Vista: London
Van Nostrand Reinhold Company:
New York

A Studio Vista/Van Nostrand Reinhold Paperback
Edited by John Lewis
©Richard Taylor 1971
Published in London by Studio Vista Limited
Blue Star House, Highgate Hill, London N19
and in New York by Van Nostrand Reinhold Publishing Company
a Division of Litton Educational Publishing, Inc.
450 West 33 Street, New York, NY 10001
Library of Congress Catalog Card Number: 79–150598
Set in 9/12 pt Univers
Printed and bound in the Netherlands
by Drukkerij Reclame N.V., Gouda
British SBN paperback 289 70106 6
              hardback   289 70107 4

Acknowledgements

I am indebted to the staff of the Departments of Graphic Design and Three-dimensional Design at Bristol Polytechnic for the material used to describe a contemporary graphic design course.
The book could not have been written without the kind, delicated and detailed assistance of Mary Lavington (Department secretary) and the full encouragement of John Lewis, not only a regular visitor to the Department, both before, during and following the events described, but also as a friend and counsellor.
I must thank, too, the various people whose writings, lectures and discussions have helped to frame my thoughts on many of the matters concerned with art and design education.

R. Taylor
Bristol 1970

Graphic design, usually thought of as a derivative of painting, was at one time called commercial art. In recent years it has moved away from this image and has emerged as a problem-solving, design activity. The graphic designer, like any other designer, is a specialist who is concerned with solving other people's problems, usually in a specifically industrial or social context. In the case of graphic design, these problems are always to do with visual communication. The graphic designer may work individually or in a group directly concerned with visual communication problems. His audience is specific and certain. By contrast, the subjective artist, concerned with self-expression and self-communication, works to constraints and problems of his own choice. His work is of necessity personal. Such observations are neither new nor conclusive.

This book, in one form or another, is concerned with illuminating the evolutionary forces which directly contribute to the design discipline of visual communication. The confusion directly related to graphic design's historic association with fine art has caused many bizarre misconceptions. (The prefix 'fine' refers to the arts of painting and sculpture, to distinguish them from the applied arts.) Functional graphics has been referred to as Marxist, Fascist and Bauhaus art — poor Bauhaus, one would think that some forty-seven years after the event, with Bauhaus relics safely behind museum glass, its ghosts were laid for ever!

Some confusions exist on the relative value of the various types of creativity that belong to the disciplines of design and art. Creativity in terms of visual aesthetics and a strongly individual style is itself often referred to as being or belonging to the same *genre* as art, whilst conceptual processes are either dismissed as being unnecessarily mixed up with the 'scaffolding' or plainly something to be left to a lower level of 'mechanical' thinking. The graphic designer is most concerned with this precise point. He cannot be a designer if he divorces himself from the creative, conceptual problem of seeking and solving or if he ignores the creative associations of cultural, commercial and sometimes traditional aesthetic values. His creativity is the sum of all these parts. Richard Guyatt's description of the graphic design activity as a mixture of head, heart and hand is basically true.[1] The designer is one of the few people left in our rapidly automated and massproduced society who has the pleasure, not only of *designing* but also of taking a very large part in the *making* of his product. Architects, product designers, exhibition and furniture designers do not always have such a personal role in the physical production of their solutions.

The graphic design activity is a large area of visual communication and problems within it may be seen as containing at the one end a large element of aesthetic loading, where the problem itself is almost entirely made up of considerations of visual appearance — problems such as wallpaper design or decorative illustration — whilst across a graphic design spectrum the degree of conscious aesthetic loading decreases to a point such as a computerised telephone bill, where the conscious aesthetic element is virtually non-existent. It is perhaps instructive to note that the actual appearance of graphic elements in the lessening aesthetic scale derive their appearance from an inverse ratio of increasingly functional considerations. Invariably, though sometimes slowly, this new functional appearance becomes a new aesthetic. The inductive process from function into aesthetic is a continuous process and is of such importance that descriptions of it could fill a book.

Most of the preliminary education leading to graphic design, being fine-art-based, is heavily biased towards both the aesthetic and the craft-based processes (and here it must be emphatically stressed that the place of art in the learning processes of the young is NOT in question). In many instances there is a complete ignorance or even an appreciation, that graphic design contains *functional* design. A glaring example of this can be seen in the 1969 Careers Booklet, published in Great Britain by H.M. Stationery Office, on 'Careers in Art and Design'. This booklet describes employment factors for 'graphic *art*' as consisting of art work for greetings cards, calendars and pictorial matter for advertisements, books, etc. Typography is treated perfunctorily whilst package design is under a separate heading altogether!

[1] *Head, heart and hand,* Richard Guyatt, Royal College of Art, 1949.

This misinformation is indicative not only of the confusion resulting from integrating art with design but also of the widespread misconception throughout our educational system. This also indicates how recent is the evolution of graphics as a *design* activity.

Tradition[2] dies hard. Consequently for many, in the present climate of dissolving subject boundaries and in recognition of the important links with man's evolution of perceptual, mental processes, it would appear downright disloyal to expound the differences between art and design. Indeed, it should be acknowledged that graphics has only itself to blame for its belated appearance as a true design discipline, since the elements that finally forced the issue have been present, in many forms, throughout the whole history of its development.

To understand the various complex influences which affect the visual appearance of objects fashioned by man requires a study of the whole history of man's development, including all art, science, psychology, philosophy, sociology and metaphysics. The list is endless and any reference to one aspect is certain to invite criticism of superficiality and historic misrepresentation. It is important, nonetheless, if a greater understanding is to be effected, to place present day graphic design and its attendant educational requirements into some degree of historical and social context. I have attempted to set an historical context by two interrelated propositions, the first being a personal appraisal of some of the forces which may be seen to govern the appearance of man-made objects and the second a brief historical survey of the development of present day graphic design.

The survey employs a major assumption[3] regarding two interwoven human attributes, namely that certain aspects of the perception and thinking processes can be regarded as having developed separate but interrelated paths. In the belief that the reader can accept this schizophrenic approach, the historical description of the growth of graphic design also requires a degree of tolerance in that since a complete history including every important event, name, motivation and style is clearly not possible, the method employed uses selective choice which carries inherent dangers of misrepresentation. However, despite the obvious perils of a stepping-stone technique – choosing the wrong

[2] Tradition – the transfer of information through non genetic channels from one generation to the next. P. M. Medawar.
[3] The reader who is troubled by the assumption may wish to consider how a blind person learns – and the general acceptance of phonetic language as the major component in man's ability to learn.

9

stones and missing larger ones below the surface – this method will at least allow a critical path, from which one can make some conclusions. There are occasional side-steps from the main direction, which are intended to give a degree of reference to period and time.

In mammals, reptiles and fish that have a developed sense of sight, the mechanism of visual signal stimulae is an essential device of regulation or control for species survival. With additional senses of hearing, touch and smell, the appearance, including that of posture of display, ensured survival by ritualised reproduction, social relationships, territorial and defence systems. In less organic terms, human social groups, sub-groups and micro-groups require a degree of group identity which has characteristics very similar to that used by species survival systems. Throughout history men have identified their allegiance to social orders and various levels of hierarchical order by such things as clothing, houses, transport and symbols. In today's complex society-structure certain social organisms are identifiable by their outside appearance. The generation gap may be marked not only by attitudes and behaviour patterns and the wearing of non-traditional or challenging clothing, but also by a form of music on a decibel scale which virtually amounts to a 'sound barrier' to older generations. Similarly the drop-out elements of young society or the 'hippy flower-power cult' has identified its image in psychedelic art, which is reputedly derived from hallucinations produced by the drug LSD. Beyond these rather obvious social observations there lies a much deeper level of collective visual experience which forms a kaleidoscope of inducted[4] visual values. These are trace elements from our developing man-made environment.

Psychedelic art, as we have noted above, derived from the hallucinations produced by LSD. During these hallucinations the participant experiences a disorientation of the sight, audio, tactile and smelling sense. He sees vivid, primitive, violent and often arresting visual patterns. This bizarre art form is linked with the cult of 'flower-power' and its associated philosophy of every human being having the right to determine his own reality. Folk music expresses this ideology. It has become synonymous with young people's concern for individual expression. The mass-produced standardised car, or any other mass-produced object, which they paint in psychedelic shapes and colours, is not only an outward expression of their concern but possibly the first visible shock wave of a changing society. It is interesting to observe

4 A transference, an influence.

how quickly the visual impact of this violent break with conservative custom is being absorbed into the norm of present day traditional appearance. It illustrates how even our current permissive society is forced to protect itself by assimilation.

The adaptation of function into a decorative form is of course valid for all other products of the human psyche, including music, poetry, costume, literature, dance forms, art and the sciences. General acceptance of value judgements results in our present day 'traditional appearance'. However, since the sixteenth century these subjective judgement values have been invested in standards called 'good taste'. In contemporary terminology it is guardedly referred to as simply 'taste' and although stoutly defying definition, 'taste' is reputed to be immediately recognisable.

In visual terms, good taste is based on the acceptance of a refined traditional appearance, always good mannered, often romantic in its conceptual appreciation of craftsmanship and historical uniqueness. It has little to do with the real issues of art and little more than a brushing acquaintance with design, as many designers know to their cost. Refined traditional appearances that survive the passage of time become cultural values that are used for judgement of all other appearances. Cultural values are of course dependent on visual education which, because of its variations, must point to questions regarding comparative aesthetics, a field of study so far almost unexplored by the psychology of perception. Is there a common link between a Ming vase, an Egyptian bas-relief, a Byzantine mosaic, a drawing by Michelangelo? Good taste would have no doubts — but how much of the quality is due initially to an economic fulfilment of a function? Is it conceivable that a vase evolved its refinement from a functional purpose and that Michelangelo, by investigating a problem by the most direct means available to him, was able to tap essential qualities of functional form? Is it just possible that all great art is great because it has captured the dynamic force lines of function? The difference between a Ming vase and a plastic cup and saucer from Woolworths may not be one primarily of good or bad taste; it could be one of function and numeracy. Two hundred years from now the first plastic cup and saucer may carry the same veneration that the Ming pot enjoys today.

Aesthetics, a natural corollary of 'good taste' must, because of its complicated nature, remain largely outside our prescribed stepping-stones. It is curious nevertheless that in common with many such complex subjects the 'obvious' is sometimes very understressed, i.e. that aesthetics are personal, comparative and relative to their time and age; that individual aesthetics relate to two integrated human attributes, perception and emotion. A botanist's knowledgeable aesthetic appreciation of a plant structure is likely to be different from that of a flower-shop assistant, whilst the flower-shop assistant, assuming she is a lover of flowers, may have a greater level of subjective perceptual appreciation. Beyond this point, if one acknowledges that perceptive sense assists the emotive process and emotional powers assist perception, the prickly path of metaphysics, philosophy and all manner of unresolved confusion begins.

The acceptance of a functional approach to certain aspects in the spectrum of graphic design is, curiously enough, resisted by many exponents of a tolerant society. Such reactions to visual appearances based on any form of logic may be rooted in subjective fears of standardisation and conformity. Appreciation of visual communication problems, be they typographic, photographic, drawn or painted, can be restricted by the tradition or by the exercise of an entirely aesthetically based judgement.

The influence of art, from which many important graphic features originated, and the authority of the researches made by the art historian and art philosopher (whose preoccupation with artistic expression often excluded the more utilitarian aspects of visual communication), together with the less obvious characteristics of traditional appearance, have succeeded in inhibiting a proper realisation of the functional needs and essential qualitative values of graphic design.

Because such largely emotional views ignore the historical trends from which functional graphics have evolved, I think it is important to outline this part of the history of graphic design before describing a contemporary approach to graphic design education.

CHAPTER 2

It is thought that the 30,000-year-old cave-paintings of Lascaux and Altamira were a focal point for primitive hunting and religious rites so they may be considered as serving a functional purpose. The service of art to religion as an interpreter and communicator of religious expressive thought continued to a point comparatively late in the history of art. The conversion from this utilitarian use to a more personal, directed means of expression did not crystallise until relatively recent times.

Being thus at the centre of human aspirations, religion and art formed the bastions of the balance between intuition and logic. The transition of art to a personal, expressive form of communication carried with it the tradition of its previous eminence and whilst no-one today would define today's art as religious communication, to most sensibilities the sanctity of the individual is of paramount importance. In these terms the art of present times, by amplifying this importance, may be said to be continuing its original role as a vehicle of philosophical, if not religious, beliefs. Art speaks across the barriers of time and, unlike any other form of communication, radiates fresh messages to the onlooker. With intuitive and logical insight it has, by accumulative steps, revealed spiritual truths regarding man's dignity and his needs beyond the physical and material elements.

Originating from the same root source as art and man's earliest communication, in the form of sign object relationships, graphics has formed the natural link between man's developing reasoning and perceptual thought patterns. The early Chinese picture-writing, pictograms, ideograms and Egyptian hieroglyphic writing give a clear indication of a breakaway utilitarian art form developing into a formal language. The full implication of graphic communication in association with language and conceptual thought is now being reassessed with the present exploration of the problems of converting typographic principles together with associated semantics, semiotics or grammorama to binary and bolean algebraic terms with which it is necessary to programme a computer. The traditional styles of present day alphabets reveal all the characteristics of earlier writing and printing techniques, including the written forms of the stylus, quill and pen, the incised or chiselled forms derived from letters cut into stone, with its relationship to Mediterranean sunlight, and flowing styles developing from engraved copper or the mild steel of armour plate.

Widespread illiteracy, as in various parts of the underdeveloped world today, still needed practical symbols in the form of heraldry and similar signs. In general, as the relatively small element of literate priesthood shows, man's thinking and perceptual powers were indivisibly linked and developed in progressive harmony. The methods of visual layout evolved by the scribes for the illuminated manuscripts and books produced a standardised format for presenting written information. The format consisted of two rectangles, the governing vertical and horizontal lines of which formed grids containing variable elements of bilateral symmetry. The rectangles containing the information developed a further aesthetic of an even tone or texture produced by even letter-, word- and interline-space. The standardised rectangle, which was to be the characteristic appearance of man's civilisation, proved also the most practical shape with which to lock up and fix separate small elements of cast-metal type. Gutenberg's invention made use of an existing method of presenting information in the form of rectangular shapes, one each on the recto and verso sides of the open book, a tradition which has lasted for over five hundred years. Illuminations in Psalters, Herbals and religious Calendars or Books of Hours, reached a high level of sophistication both before and after the introduction of printing from moveable type. Certain aspects of our present day graphic design were evolved from these informative images.

In addition to book illustrations, separate visualisation in the form of drawing was bound up with the making of things, as a means of fixing the potential shape or geometry of a proposed structure. The earliest known example of this form of graphic communication is the representation of a drawing board incised into the stone base of the statue of Gudea of Ur dated 2130 BC. A board in the Louvre Museum shows a ground plan of a temple together with a scribing instrument and 'scale' and reveals how slowly man's technology moved in subsequent civilisations. Vitruvius's *Ten Books on Architecture,* from the time of the early Renaissance to the present day, has had an enormous influence on architecture. It was written about twenty-five years before the birth of Christ and contains drawing techniques of plans and elevations not only for buildings and water-lifting devices but also for rudimentary machinery. In general, however, it is unlikely that machines were designed on papyrus, vellum or paper before the time of Valturius and da Vinci, since the process of craftsmanship, which was in step with the known technology, evolved from a father-to-son communication. Such drawings as the craftsman did use, employing the instruments of straight edge, square and compass which are still the basic tools of present-day draughtsmen, consisted of marking-out procedures on the construction materials. Eventually, with the advent of the trade guild system, these skills were to disappear behind veils of secrecy.

The first known system for projecting plan and elevation into a three-dimensional projection, intended for artists rather than craftsmen, was published by Albrecht Dürer in 1528. The system, based on a modular of a man's height and incorporating laws of perspective, waited upon the advances of the geometers and astronomers for its measured mathematical expression.

The effect of printing with its relatively rapid spread of literacy hastened the developing divisions between aspects of conceptual and perceptual thought. The illustrated book with factual illustrations was mainly northern European in origin. In general the classical scholars and humanists of the Italian Renaissance regarded illustration as being suitable only for the 'vulgar and illiterate'. In localised areas of learning, and depending on the nature of the book, illustrative matter, in the form of printed woodcuts, either disappeared altogether or remained as a decorative feature – often completely irrelevant blocks were placed in a text to satisfy, perhaps for reasons of prestige. Popular subject matter such as Aesop's *Fables,* Herbals and other semi-text-books contained factual illustrations which served as visual aids for the semi-literate and illiterate alike.

The earliest known printed technical illustrations are those of Robert Valturius, who produced woodcuts of naval and military equipment in a handbook for military leaders of the Renaissance. Printed in 1472, it is known that Leonardo da Vinci possessed a copy whilst acting as chief engineer to Caesar Borgia. Michelangelo and Leonardo da Vinci perhaps underline the general affinity between thought and perception, or science and art; there were of course many indications of the impending division, perhaps foretold by Desiderius Erasmus, who, in his dialogues, promoted a rationalism to which fanaticism and tyranny were both abhorrent. The utilitarian nature of printing made it a servant of art and many famous artists began their early training or instruction in the engraving workshops of the craft printer.

From its beginnings on the banks of the Rhine, printing spread to all areas of the civilised world and was, together with the art of painting, the vehicle of man's understanding and expression and the revelation of his spiritual aspirations. Art, whilst equally forming man's development, sought to 'reveal and understand' by its inherent perceptual powers. Areas of the world, however, that remained uninfluenced by the spread of printing and knowledge,[2] remained underdeveloped until almost recent times. In these isolated communities art remained virtually unchanged as an elemental homeostatic force directly contributing to the status quo.

Parallel with the printed book and in the growing complexity of developing social needs, graphic communication also existed in a variety of forms of printed ephemera and in maps, plans, elevations, charts and diagrams for the sciences, thereby underlining the special importance of graphic communication as a vehicle for instant and accurate comprehension. The spoken and printed word can never be a universal norm of complete understanding since their values are open to various degrees of interpretation. Apart from numerical order — and even here discrepancies occasionally occur — graphics, especially technical graphics, have produced instant and assessable information. This is indicative of man's essential dependability on graphic communication. Man's socio-development has not run an even course. The part played by the guilds in relation to certain graphic restrictions and usage is, however, relevant. The guilds system, with its imposed vows of secrecy, prevented the exchange of information on techniques, on instruction and on graphic communication for engineers, builders, shipwrights, instrument makers and other craftsmen of the 18th century. However, as an example of good graphics, the guilds displayed a corporate image or visual device which, in addition to revealing their particular activity, also performed a function of persuasive communication, which helped to ensure individual identification and allegiance. The 'Age of Reason' realised the vital divisions between art, religion and logic. As early as 1780 James Watt had introduced standardised interchangeable machine parts and by 1798 mass production of inter-

[2] It was the use of phonetic alphabet which allowed printing to develop. Picture language countries remained without print and without development, i.e. Korea.

changeable machine parts for armaments had begun in the United States. Such beginnings of mass production and subsequent division of labour were not, because of the practices of the guilds system, based on the remotest suggestion of standardised practices of engineering drawing and were based entirely on templates and gauges made by craftsmen from a prototype.

In *An Essay on the Principles of Population,* published in 1798, Thomas Malthus stated that population increases at a greater rate than the means of subsistence and held that checks on the growth of population would be necessary — a prophesy that exercised a strong influence, not merely on economics but on all social theory. Significantly, two years later, the first human assembly-line appeared in the Royal Navy victualling yard at Deptford, to be replaced by a roller system by the 1830's.

With the final passing of the Abolition of Slavery Act in 1833, William Wilberforce realised his life's ambition. The slave trade had been abolished in 1807 and the presentation to the House of Commons of a technical, diagrammatic deck plan of a slave ship, showing the storage of the chained slaves, is perhaps a very early example of how immensely persuasive statistical graphics could be.

Joshua Reynolds and Thomas Gainsborough painted the romantic setting and the countryside of the upper classes of the day, whilst Watteau and Fragonard perpetuated the French aristocratic dream. Following Goya's example, Blake and Hogarth used the graphic printing media of etching and engraving as a method of protest against the conditions of the time. *This fusion of socially conscious art on to graphic media of reproduction may be considered as one of the main reasons why graphics developed in the 19th and 20th centuries as a derivate of art, if not as an actual art form in itself.*

CHAPTER 3

The accelerating industrial revolution of production and its consequent increased concentrations of population, together with an emergent middle class, produced new requirements, not only for advertising and books, but all manner of graphic communication in the form of papers, almanacks, broadsheets and magazines. Technical developments in printing resulted in a sharp fall in the standards of printing craftsmanship. One of the first to react against this was William Morris, who in the last years of his life set out to re-establish medieval qualities of craftsmanship in the productions of the Kelmscott Press. From today's vantage point it is revealing that, despite Morris's aims, all the productions from the Kelmscott Press are unmistakably late-Victorian in appearance. The search for values in craftsmanship and the close association with art may have become stumbling blocks to function. Paradoxically, it was the unfulfilled Morris concepts that directly influenced the modern movement in design. His historical understanding of what he was doing in a machine age meant a re-vitalising of forces already in existence. Herman Muthesius, whose experience in England and association with W. R. Lethaby, the Principal of the London Central School of Arts and Crafts, led to the setting up of similar schools in Germany, Austria, Switzerland and Scandinavia. Directors of these schools, such as Peter Behrens, Van de Velde and Bruno Paul, already stimulated by the English Arts and Crafts movement, were to become important architects of the modern movement.

By 1914, Constructivism and Suprematism, two movements of abstract art, were firmly established as major developments of Cubism and Futurism, the movements which had romanticised the machine. The Bolshevik revolution of 1917 with its vision of a new society transformed by industrialisation and a promise of an integrated communal life for the artist (a concept that disappeared in the Middle Ages), gave the new abstract artists a higher sense of reality and practical purpose.

Ousting the traditional and academic easel painters, the Constructivists, headed by Vladimir Tatlin, and the Suprematists by Kasimir Malevich, became the 'official art' in the first four years of the revolution. Constructivism, previously called Production Art, carried an emphasis on technique which was to replace style of any kind and those Constructivists who pursued the artist-engineer philosophy found the disciplines of graphic communication to be the most suited to the use of modern technology. Thus Rodchenko, Klutsis, Alexei Gan and Lissitzky worked out pioneer examples of functional typographic design which, together with use of photography and photographic montage, revolutionised these forms of communication.

Lissitzky, initially trained as a civil engineer and architect, combined both Constructivist and Suprematist principles in his graphic communication and it was he, more than any other artist or designer, who acted as a link between Russia and Western Europe.

The appointment of Walter Gropius to the newly formed Weimar Staatliches Bauhaus, a combination of art school, trade workshop and laboratory, took place in 1919. The Bauhaus became for over a decade a catalyst of the interacting forces from Russia, Holland, Switzerland and Italy. Most of these heady developments were built on the English Arts and Crafts Movement and the pre-war German Werkbund.

As early at 1909 Gropius, a pupil of Behrens, had carried out a memorandum on standardisation and mass production of small houses. Such buildings as the Fagus factory in 1911 and the model factory for the Werkbund exhibition at Cologne in 1914, designed by Gropius and Meyer, were a synthesis of organic architecture and modern technology and vastly ahead of their time.

In Germany, the unstable political climate following the 1914 war led to the Bauhaus being regarded by many as a hot-bed of cultural Bolshevism. The aim of the Bauhaus was somewhat different. It was repeated by Gropius in 1955. He recalls:

'Thus the Bauhaus was inaugurated in 1919 with the specific object of realising a modern architectonic art, which like human nature was meant to be all-embracing in its scope. It deliberately concentrated primarily on what has now become a work of imperative urgency — averting mankind's enslavement by the machine by saving the mass product and the home from mechanical anarchy and by restoring them to purpose, sense and life. This means evolving goods and buildings specifically designed for industrial reproduction. Our object was to eliminate the drawbacks of the machine without sacrificing any one of its real advantages. We aimed at realizing standards of excellence, not creating transient novelties. Experiment once more became the centre of architecture, and that demands a broad, co-ordinating mind, not the narrow specialist.

What the Bauhaus preached in practice was the common citizenship of all forms of creative work, and their logical interdependence on one another in the modern world. Our guiding principle was that design is neither an intellectual nor a material affair, but simply an integral part of the stuff of life, necessary for everyone in a civilised society. Our ambition was to rouse the creative artist from his other-worldliness and reintegrate him into the workaday world of realities and, at the same time, to broaden and humanise the rigid, almost exclusive material mind of the businessman. Our conception of the basic unity of design in relation to life was in diametric opposition to that of 'art for art's sake' and the much more dangerous philosophy it sprang from, 'business as an end in itself'.

This explains our concentration on the design of technical products and the organic sequence of their process of manufacture, which gave rise to an erroneous idea that the Bauhaus had set itself up as the apotheosis of rationalism.' . . .

Between 1919 and 1922, Bauhaus teaching reflected the influence of Futurism, Dadaism and particularly the Dutch de Stijl movement through the teaching of Theo van Doesburg. By calling on the exponents of abstract and Cubist painting such as Kandinsky, Feininger, Klee and Schlemmer, Gropius sought to create an experimental environment that would be a basis for a new architecture.

The Constructivist Congress at Dusseldorf in 1922 led by Lissitzky and Ehrenburg, had a marked influence on the Bauhaus and with the appointment of the Hungarian Constructivist László Moholy-Nagy and Joseph Albers to the school, Russian Constructivism became a potent teaching method. Functionalism became a creative force in the Bauhaus with the introduction of Russian Constructivism.

Moholy-Nagy, friend and follower of Lissitzky, made the greatest contribution to the development of a new typographic style, used in conjunction with photography. The typography produced at the Bauhaus by Moholy-Nagy and his colleagues was to be of the greatest importance to the future of graphic design. Its logic revealed a new process for function, hitherto believed to be a part of the processes of art and craft. Whilst the aesthetics of Bauhaus architecture, furniture and artifacts could be appreciated as the result of their 'interior' function, graphics depended upon a much more subtle condition of conceptual appreciation. The uninitiated could see how a Mies van der Rohe chair worked but a typographical layout could easily be mistaken for a simplified, modern visual trick. Similarly, the Constructivist and Dadaist-Surrealist's use of photo-montage had a great influence on the contemporary scene. The Constructivists sought to rationalise everything and used photo-montage to amplify visual reality. They despised the Dada-Surrealist approach that used photo-montage intuitively, relying on the subjective values of the subconscious to destroy the appearance of reality.

In various parts of Europe the use of traditional photographic representation and static typography gave way, in the mid-twenties, to a more dynamic presentation. In Italy the Futurist abstract art evolved new photographic methods, whilst in Germany and Holland photo-montage was used equally in political and commercial advertising.

The American approach to advertising, which had moved away from the application of popularised or 'commercial' art, evolved out of fierce competition between large corporations involved with producing similar articles for mass consumption. The Young and Rubicon Agency employed George Gallup to do mass research on consumer consumption and then used the information to create a safe selling method as as early as 1937. The stimulus of competition between large companies selling the same product meant, in the late fifties when many firms had amalgamated, the continuation of a completely false element of competitive advertising. Undue or over-applied use of the newly discovered 'socio-economic group' factor and subliminal sales techniques heralded dangers not only to the advertising industry itself — which must surely depend on free choice of the individual — but also to our whole economic way of life. In addition, possibly equally well realised, the development of photographic, cinematic and television technology is effecting changes in every aspect of our values and environment. It is hardly surprising that students began to question our way of life. Despite all this, and the growth of many small design groups and consultancies, the advertising industry is still probably the largest single employer of graphic designers. In an advertising agency today the graphic designer does not produce commercial art — which for our purposes we will define as art work for no specific problem — he is essentially a specialist in a team with a variety of skills in the disciplines of visual communication.

Because of the apparent realism of photography, film and television media, the amount of planning and preparatory design work involved with this form of communication is often under-estimated. The camera cannot automatically record concepts, it requires controlled visual planning, economy and a mastery of the disciplines of sequence, time, motion and technical know-how. The graphic designer, whose abilities allow for the versatile use of many disciplines to a single concept of communication, is naturally suited to the use of this medium.

In film and television, where art and design are inexorably intertwined, the contributions of the film producer, the film director, designer and camera man must be seen as parts of a creative whole. In the strictest sense, therefore, it is difficult to regard such composite activity as an 'art form'. On the other hand, such concepts as symbolism, montage, the absence of real-life space-time-continuum, spatial order, etc., have their direct roots in abstract art.

As with many other visual media, it is in the graphic designer's use of the cine or television camera as a graphic tool that the main differences between art and design may be drawn. Designers in this field, apart from being proficient in traditional graphic disciplines and many aspects of construction design, familiarises himself with technical problems unique to this medium.

Two other important stepping-stones affecting graphic communication, that developed between the two wars, were engineering-drawing practice and the psychology of perception.

Engineering-drawing practice, which since 1850 had borrowed certain techniques from architecture and civil engineering; those which employed colour as a means of illustrating the potential impression and later as a means of coding and various materials, gave way to the use of the blueprint in the face of increasing complexities of materials and information to be recorded. Various projection systems involving an arrangement of projected views, necessary for clear interpretation, crystallised in America to a standardised third-angle technique. A problem, possibly unique to engineering drawing, of representing by a unified code the techniques of fits and tolerances for interchange-ability for manufacture and organisation remain unsolved.

The second stepping-stone started with M. W. Wertheimer's psycholo-gical theory of the Gestalt which had in 1912 challenged the psycholo-gical theories of behaviourism and introspective functionalism. By the time (1935) Kofka produced his *Principles of Gestalt Psychology* – or the psychology of perception, its position as a major theory had largely ousted all other concepts. It was to have a major influence on all enquiries into visual phenomena for the next forty years.

CHAPTER 4

In the 1940's, visual aids imposed by the massive training and retraining problems of a technological war made great advances and found unlikely areas of use in such elements as Walt Disney's film animation techniques. Apart from technological advances, a common feature of all wars (and perhaps the main reason for man's rapid technology advance), the enforced economy brought about other advances which were to have a great influence in later years; features that are now affecting concepts of traditional subject boundaries. A passage from Eric Duckworth's *Introduction to Operational Research* 1969, which is an outline of a common language for all scientific specialisms, may assist the point:

> 'When the British Government, anxious not to waste resources in the years following Dunkirk, banded together groups of scientists to assist field commanders in solving strategic problems, it caused biologists to examine problems in electronics, physicists to observe movements of men rather than movements of molecules, mathematicians to examine how probability theory could influence men's survival and chemists to study equilibria in systems other than chemical ones. Similar work was being done under the Chief Scientist of the U.S.A. War Department. From all this work arose the realisation that techniques for studying systems in one discipline could be used with success in solving problems outside that discipline.'

The development in 1949 of *Information Theory* by two doctors, Claude Shannon and Warren Weaver, arose from the problems involved with many simultaneous telephone conversations transmitted over the same cable. The central problem here was to find a measure to describe numerically the amount of information in a message, then to isolate disturbing influences (noise) and to process the information in the receiver. This investigation of the flow of information, i.e. transmitter to receiver, led to the theory of data processing, feedback systems and general communication theory, from which there is growing a *greater understanding of all human communication*. Semiotics[1], probability theory and programmed teaching systems are directly concerned with this development.

By the mid-fifties the ever-increasing acceleration of technology, the associated stresses of social reorganisation and the adjustments due to the first indications of automation and population increase, together with the natural outcome of a competitive economy, the 'takeover bid' and the consequent Monopolies Commission, the recognition of a teen-age market, jet travel, atom- and hydrogen-bomb testing and rising radiation levels, individual possession of the automobile and the television set, all these factors brought pressures on a system whose structure and communications systems were still emerging from the horsebuggy and steam locomotive era. Out of the Welfare State grew a society from which there appeared a growing, socially destructive force of materialism. Operating in the near chaos of informative excesses, American and British business techniques and associated advertising know-how asserted an ever-increasing persuasion based on market research, subliminal techniques derived from psychology of perception, humour and all-pervading sex.

The merging of large separate industries produced the need for new images. A streamlining of the internal communication systems drove the graphic designer into systems analysis and management techniques. The more successful corporate device (sometimes based on the house style which had its roots in all previous heraldic symbolism) was usually simple, logical and capable of adaption to all applications of the commercial market. These often ranged from a minute swing label, sticker or letterhead to the marking on vehicles and aircraft. Two or three letters were often combined and geometrical associated image which effected a 'recall' of the companies' acitivities. This too, whilst not aspiring to the persuasive character of historic symbolism, possessed the clear functional identity necessary to cut through all the visual clutter.

[1] It is not intended to ignore the foundation work by Willard Gibbs, Bolzman and the publication of *Cybernetics* in 1948 (Norbert Weiner).
'The word cybernetics — roughly meaning steersmanship or the science of control and communication in the animal and machine, was not introduced in its modern sense until 1947; the ideas involved had been put forward and developed in previous years by a group of scientists, including Weiner. Weiner himself was working at this time on the design of a computational device for use in anti-aircraft warfare and noticed that some of the principles that he was using could apparently be applied to the description of certain aspects of human behaviour as well.' Dr Michael Apter. Recall Vol 1. January 1969.

These sudden changes in our surroundings and in particular in the way commerce was making use of graphic design, caused a number of people to question just what their function as graphic designers should be. A few leading graphic designers, who, since the 1939–45 war had produced levels of graphic communication revealing an insight into functional and cultural values managed to remain aloof from the 'exploitation at any price' philosophy. The concern for the manner in which graphic designers were being asked to commit themselves was reflected in a 'Manifesto' by some British graphic designers. This statement was headed "First Things First". It read thus:

'We the undersigned, are graphic designers, photographers and students who have been brought up in a world in which the techniques and apparatus of advertising have persistently been presented to us as the most lucrative, effective and desirable means of using our talents. We have been bombarded with publications devoted to this belief, applauding the work of those who have flogged their skill and imagination to sell such things as:
cat food, stomach powders, detergents, hair restorer, striped tooth paste, after-shave lotion, before-shave lotion, slimming diets, fattening diets, deodorants, fizzwater, cigarettes, roll-ons, pull-ons and slip-ons.
By far the greatest time and effort of those working in the advertising industry are wasted on these trivial purposes, which contribute little or nothing to our national prosperity. In common with an increasing number of the general public, we have reached saturation point at which the high pitched scream of consumer selling is no more than sheer noise. We think that there are other things more worth using our skill and experience on. There are the signs for streets and buildings, books and periodicals, catalogues, instructional manuals, industrial photography, educational aids, films, television features, scientific and industrial publications and all other media through which we promote our trade, our education, our culture and our great awareness of the world.
We do not advocate the abolition of high pressure consumer advertising: this is not feasible. Nor do we want to take any fun out of life. But we are proposing a reversal of priorities in favour of the more useful and more lasting forms of communication. We hope that our society will tire of gimmick merchantry, status salesman and hidden persuaders, and that the prior call on our skills will be for worthwhile purposes. With this in mind, we propose to share our experience and opinions, and to make them available to colleagues, students and others who may be interested.'
Published by Ken Garland in 1964 and signed by twenty-two graphic designers, photographers and students.

'Designers of the World unite, you have nothing to lose but your chains!' – Duncan.

The design school 'The Hochschule für Gestaltung', at Ulm, came into being in 1950; initially directed by Max Bill, who had been a student at the Bauhaus, Bill was followed by Tomas Maldonado as Principal in 1955. By the late fifties it became apparent to the outside world that Ulm, whilst having certain links with Bauhaus by way of visiting staff (several of whom were previous members of Bauhaus), was a quite unique design school. The methods used at Ulm were almost entirely analytical and whilst most of its activity was concerned with modern industrial design, its systems and processes promoted a socio-design philosophy related to environmental design, calling for a 'humanised science'. Concerned with analysis, methodology and enquiry, Ulm revealed a scientifically-based way of thinking that separated it from the main premise of present day subjective art. *Upon the nature of the design situation, the allocation of the intuitive process either to a limited area in the design process or its outright rejection as a valid concept meant, dependent upon one's individual viewpoint, that the umbilical cord generally conceded to exist between art and design was now either completely severed or at the least severely stretched.*

In retrospect (the enforced closure of Ulm occurred in 1968), the devastating message from Ulm was, quite simply, 'Chaos or order' — and if the choice is order then designers should be to the forefront of its human formulation and its future guardian.

Because of its nature and purpose Ulm could not, and did not, produce a new aesthetic for graphic design — and for those who evaluate graphic values by this criterion alone this was confirmation of what they regarded as sterility. Superficial aspects of the first year teaching methods employed in the visual communication department at Ulm filtered through to the 'image hunters' as a new style, but these became so infused with the vogue of Op Art that they were of little influence. The search for a systematic common visual language for the dynamic forms of abstract art dated back to Johannes Itten's famous 'Basic Course' at the Bauhaus and to such treatises as *Language of Vision* by Gyorgy Kepes, *The Thinking Eye* by Paul Klee and many others, which were finally summarized in *Basic Design: the dynamics of visual form* by Maurice de Sausmarez in 1964.

This partial formulation of a language of aesthetics and creativity in aesthetics held sway in most 'up-to-date' art and design schools and formed a starting point for many so-called basic design courses. In many instances, as with Harry Thrubron's course at Leeds, it provided an intense stimulus to the awakening of a student's visual awareness. In some other cases, however, its values became a moribund orthodoxy a fashionable and easy way out for the design teacher. Such must be the danger of all text books! In the long run, common visual language for art and design may exist and the works mentioned uncovered and delineated many viable aspects of this unknown ground. Whilst in the right hands it is a potent teaching method, it cannot be regarded as *the basis of all art and design*.

'The design process', a refinement of design methodology, produced by Ulm in the mid sixties, had existed throughout design centres in different parts of the world, its direct parentage being the methodology used throughout the natural sciences — a human way of working that will increasingly change many aspects of the look of graphics. It is a dynamism which cannot forseeably be distorted by the world of fashion and style.

Swiss typographic methods, which had developed as a direct link with the Bauhaus and from the writings of Tschichold and the work of Max Bill, were integral with the Ulm way of thinking. The wide influence of the typeface Univers, designed by Adrian Frutiger, originated outside the Ulm environment. Planned in four weights and four widths, giving a total range of twenty-one sizes, it was the first typeface in five hundred years of printing history to be designed as a complete and related family before a single matrix was cut. Univers was initially released for film setting by Lumitype for the magazine *Paris Match,* with optimum consideration for distortions caused by enlargement and reduction etc. It was re-issued by Monotype in 1961. Frutiger, in the following year's *Penrose Annual* wrote:

> 'Our own age seems to have found its expression in concrete, but modern concrete buildings are not just geometrical; the forms have become supple and alive. Construction on geometrical foundations, a type character must be allowed free play in its lines, thus enabling the different letters to harmonize in their expression and to endow the word, the line and the page with coherent structure.'

The general pattern of the sixties (and without the perspective of a time scale even generalities are difficult) brought a telescoping of many demands of an industrial and social nature and this is, as we are all probably aware, due to the increase in the acceleration of technology, particularly seen in the computer development, mass media communication, automation and population spread, with attendant features of generation gaps, educational unrest, immigrant adjustment and all the problems associated with a transitional environment.

Op Art, which had utilised various visual phenomena known as Newton rings or moiré patterns and later developed as a visual measuring device by engineers in observations on moving wheels, axles, etc., discovered so long ago by Isaac Newton and apparent in the early cinema and photography, had a parallel development in Pop Art, which, whilst reflecting subjective values of personal expression and the kaleidoscope of our time, relied implicitly on a low cultural level of graphic ephemera. This appeared to reduce art to the level of the narrative paintings of Victorian times. Some critics thought of it as the betrayal if not the death of painting itself. *From the graphic point of view it seemed to indicate the final abandonment of painting as a guiding force* in the field of visual thought and aesthetics since by following painting, those aspects of graphics requiring the illustrative image would be using an immolation of certain areas of its own history! For many people, understandably guided by the tradition of the historical association of art and design, it meant the fusion of art and graphic design. It is an interesting phenomenon that at precisely the same time that graphic design became consciously aware of its *real* implications as a visual communicator and also of its essential unity with all other design activities, painting assumed the guise of debased graphics! The ensuing conflicts in art and design educational establishments caused by philosophical beliefs and traditional loyalties aroused a conflagration of opposing and interacting forces, mostly ranged around concepts of intuition and logic in relation to creativity.

The overshadow of the approaching 21st century and its effect on our life and education may possibly have produced over-anxious prophesies. However, the writings of John Vaizey, the Swann and Dainton reports, together with a considerable body of opinion suggest that population increase and accelerating technology could cause a chaos that would make "Huxley's *Brave New World* and Orwell's *1984* seem like promises of salvation."[2] However, Professor Miller, in the same book, states his case for optimism — "Automation does not mean future unemployment. What it does mean, however, is a redistribution of our working forces into new occupations, with all the attendant social stress that such a shift always generates. The demands that this shift will place on our educational system are, of course, staggering — but not impossible to meet if we foresee them and begin to plan for them immediately". It would seem foolhardy and perilous indeed to dismiss *all* such forecasts as so much 'American and British chromium-plated thinking';

[2] *Psychology of Communication* by Professor George Miller.

however, whilst Marshall McLuhan has drawn our attention to the effects of the television medium[3], conclusions drawn by some people that we shall all live an automated existence via the television set by the next decade or two are frankly ridiculous. Similarly, conclusions drawn from McLuhan's *Mechanical Bride* and *Gutenberg Galaxy* that the typographic age is now over, give the impression that some educationalists live in outer space! The transition from the typographic situation to the screen may very possibly take place but is as likely to happen in our lifetime — or in that of our children who will be adults in the 21st century — as that we shall all have heart transplants and live for ever.

The logics involved in typography and the methodology of the design process have infiltrated the preconceptions, assumptions and subjective, decayed craft practices of graphic design. For those in graphic design education it has meant that, if one was so initiated or inclined (and for many it is still a doubtful hypothesis), a realisation of the importance of graphic design's 'other heritage' which, whilst including all the names traditionally included by art historians, must surely also include such concepts as Mercator's projection in 1595, Kepler, Galileo, Monge, and indeed all the graphic communicators involved in the history of science and the natural sciences. Also — and possibly more importantly — its essentially unified role for the future in education, social requirements and science, as well as its continuing traditional functional role in advertising and industry. Already its impact on our roads and motorways in the form of internationally standardised symbols which are reminiscent of the earliest graphic signs or 'pictograms' is an indication of graphic design's essentially international (and universal) communication importance.

An internationally standardised code for engineering drawing practice, relating to interchangeability and tolerance data, enabled various parts of aircraft, such as the Concorde, together with aspects of space travel technology, cars, tractors and electronics, to be manufactured in several different countries at the same time. This precise definition was only attainable by a graphic code, representing the final stages of the transference of full responsibility from the craftsman to the designer. At length the full implications and the importance of graphic communication are beginning to be realised — and particularly by educationalists.

---

[3] *Understanding Media* and *Medium is the Message*.

This educational awakening came about as a result of the pressures of the sixties. Without these pressures its slow evolutionary progress from a role aptly defined by B. R. Haydon in 1837 as 'a training in the lowest branches of art', would have continued along the same old lines. The probable result would have been that education, industry, science and advertising would have produced their own graphic designers. This is something that happens already.

With the inescapable pressures in the Western world of a colossal re-education and re-training programme, it would seem a reasonable assessment in connection with the future role of a graphic designer, that his education and training should be versatile in all the visual communication techniques, whilst also obeying specialist requirements for present day industry. It looks as if we are required to produce a two-headed monster. A man for all seasons, the full man of the Renaissance but in 20th century terms, and a vocational specialist as well. It is asking a lot of the graphic design teacher. It may put an intolerable burden on the student. Yet the choice facing all graphic design educational establishments is whether they wish to acknowledge the needs and requirements of our time and age or prefer to continue the emphasis on subjective study, producing stylists for an overcrowded market, particularly an advertising market which is subject to the winds of fashion and redundancy.

In practice, all graphic design communication requires a knowledge and experience in problem-solving and the design-process, and an education of the mind and a training of the hand based on all available modern knowledge and practice. It follows, therefore, that an education in graphic design should include design methodology, psychology of perception, with its attendant techniques of eye flows, signal strengths, Gestalt[4] theory, etc., semiotics, information theory and aspects of cybernetics, together with typography and problems associated with computer programming, photography, technical and objective drawing, printing processes and design management.

Many other subjects could be added to the list of requirements necessary for the education and training of a graphic designer; however, the concern regarding creativity and aesthetics in design in relation to fears and suspicions associated with mechanical thinking, looms large in our collective consciousness and so it would seem

4 Gestalt — a shape or structure which as an object of perception forms a specific wholly incapable of explanation simply in terms of its parts.

expedient to examine these aspects before we take a look at such additional subjects as may be revealed in some of the projects used in graphic design education in at least one school of design.[5]

[5] Department of Graphic Design in the Faculty of Art and Design at Bristol Polytechnic.

CHAPTER 5

The pressures on our present day society, which contains the computer and as many living scientists as existed in the whole of man's previous history, are such that our future society will increasingly require further degrees of standardisation and automation. This may seem a pretty depressing outlook, particularly the possibility of establishing a social system with the characteristics of a beehive. Whilst the dangers of this are real enough, an emotional overaction to *all forms* of standardisation might well promote a state of chaos.

Designers tend to believe that standardisation forms an impediment to creativity and offers a constraint to be avoided at all times. Not only is such a view unrealistic in the light of society's increasing technology and population increase, it is also historically inaccurate. Our basic languages of communication, including music, dance and mathematics are based on highly disciplined formalised rules and the standardised human form has not inhibited costume designers from producing the highest variants of creativity. Man has always lived under socially standardised patterns.

The International Standards Organisation (I.S.O.), which is concerned with correlating essential elements of world wide usage, is only at the very beginning of its immense task. Primary levels of standardistion in measurement are as yet only partially realised; the metre has three different physical measurements; there are five separate and irreconcilable typographic measures; there are endless variations in paper sizes, and so on.

Far from being able to ignore the system, the designer must be aware of all the latest standards relevant to his problem and be continuously alert to their relevance. Emotional associations with the word standardisation therefore are, for the most part, premature. It is the standards of our standardisation that should be examined, since it is these that are affecting and will increasingly affect our environment.

The resources with which man can create his environment now include the computer. The control of this machine must be our immediate concern, as the computer, with its associated science of cybernetics, uncovers a force not only for a human life without drudgery but also for a dehumanised existence. Norbert Wiener, founder of the science of cybernetics, throws some light on this paradox in his book *The Human Use of Human Beings*. In the light of this paradox no-one should remain aloof or detached from his new responsibilities. Concerned with the environment, the designer must develop his sense of logic and refine his value judgements to ensure that cultural levels are maintained.

As most school boys are aware (and many of them are already skilled programmers), a computer requires a certain type of methodology which takes the form of an alpha-numeric language for its correct use and function. It cannot be programmed by intuition — which is just as well since if this were feasible, science fiction would be a reality tomorrow; the thing is only a glorified adding machine with a built-in filing cabinet. The use of this methodology or code, even in the most mundane data processing problem, has shown extraordinary values quite unsuspected in a binary, or zero-and-one logic. From this system, somewhat more complicated than one and one makes two, certain methods of organising complex information have evolved: methods such as flow charts, algorithms, logical trees and rank order charts, all of which are now incorporated in the problem-solving designer's working methods.

Philosophical arguments against this necessity look a bit like the arguments from a dinosaur or a dodo, since such methodology rarely eliminates the intuitive element, but simply confines it to an appropriate area or place. Indeed, *there is nothing to stop anyone from measuring his intuitions* against the complex design methodology at any time, or in any circumstance.

Exponents of intuition, in the most perverse manifestations, behave as if a deity forms part of their creative subconscious or intuitive circuitry, whilst devotees of the rationale, equally perverse, hold that their cold mechanical logic is not only a human attribute by which man attempts to measure, define and comprehend the laws of the universe, but is of itself an essential part of that law.

Because of the historic infusion of art with religious thought, the term religion being implied in its widest sense, many people hold that creativity in great art is synonymous with a godlike attribute, which may possibly help to explain the deep conviction and emotion that is frequently aroused when its values and function are under discussion. The champions of logic, however, operate in a no less Olympian spirit. The metaphysics of George Berkeley in the *Principles of Human Knowledge* published in 1710, expounded his principle "that an object does not exist without a mind to perceive it" — the extension of the theory being that a mind must be the spring of the universe.

From Berkeley's metaphysics, Gottfried Wilhelm Leibnitz developed a system of philosophy with close connections with physics and mathematics, an influence that has persisted to our present day and particularly in Bertrand Russell's and Professor Whitehead's attempts to develop a systematic logic as a basis of all scientific thought.

Design methodology, a systematic way of thought, borrowed much from the rationale of science and planning office procedures, was a feature of the teaching of Hans Meyer at the Bauhaus. Together with certain architectural philosophies from before the first world war, expressed in Louis Sullivan's famous remark "Form follows Function", the synthesis of design methods gradually crystallised into the "Design Process" in the early sixties at Ulm. Self-styled as "the city of methodology", the HfG (Ulm) approach to design was for many no more than a new variant of the *furore teutonicus* — cold scrupulous, humourless, niggardly and obstinate. Others considered the HfG a more or less successful synthesis of science and design.

Several interpretations of the number of steps or sequences contained in the design process stem from several sources. Bruce Archer's method of six stages borrows from systematic methods used in organisational research and planning techniques from computer planning, whereas others are influenced by mathematics and set theory. Archer, who in recent years modified his approach to design methodology, described his six stages of the use of the design process as "a creative sandwich; the bread may be thick or thin, but the creative act is always there in the middle, however much objective and systematic analysis takes place before or after". Arguments about the stages and usage of the design process have continued with increasing fervour since the publication of Archer's series of articles *Systematic Methods of Designers* in 1963/64 and Christopher Alexander's book *Notes on the Synthesis of Form,* published in Cambridge in 1964.

The six stages of Archer's method, published, are:

1. Programming
2. Data collection
3. Analysis
4. Synthesis
5. Development
6. Communication

whilst, for comparison, the thirteen stages of J. N. Siddall, designer/engineer, amongst many variants, may serve:

1. Definition of problem
2. Scanning of all possible design and environmental variables acting on the machine
3. Definition of constraints (legal requirements and standards) uniting of design specifications
4. Creating the basic concept
5. Analysis of the evolutionary basis of the machine
6. Survey on suppliers
7. Optimization
8. Detailing
9. Calculation
10. Procurement
11. Prototypes
12. Testing

13. Final changes for Production

In design terms (and in spite of the jargon), the sequences of the design process are human, whilst being organised and flexible. Mechanical operations are only attainable by a machine, particularly the computer. Designers who attempt to apply themselves in this way, assuming it to be humanly possible, would inevitably be carrying out an automated formula and not a creative 'designing' activity.

In order to explain how a design process may be seen to work, or applied, the following description, which owes much to Norman Potter's design philosophy, may serve partially to quieten, if not dispel, certain fears regarding a suspected automated scientific design idolatry:

'The designer's special concern is other people's problems, his clients are those seeking his special skills and services. Arising from this need the designer's first responsibility is accurately to assess and possibly redefine the client's problem, since it may be confused, inaccurate, or coloured with preconceptions and false economics.'

The method of appraisal used by the designer, whether the client is clear about his problem or not, and regardless of the problem's character or type, is a gathering of all relevant information from every possible source. This process is rarely an automatic procedure, since the designer's selective or diagnostic powers are human and are as important as any part of the process. An omission at this point may affect the whole proceedings and even wreck the outcome.

The designer may seem to be clinical, factual and objective, but as he is a human being and not a computer, his objectivity must of necessity be coloured both by his experience and by the impressions he has gained from studying the problem. At this point, with all data collected (depending on the nature of the problem) the designer may find himself in a position to assess the validity of the *stated* problem. As an instance of this, and as an example not to be taken too seriously, an engineer commissioned to produce an improved specific mousetrap may have discovered that a better way of disposing of mice might be the use of poison — or upon further investigation he may have asked himself why the mice were present at all — and finally he may have come to the conclusion that the presence of mice was the client's real problem and instead of mousetraps the solution lay in better refuse disposal facilities! Obviously not all clients are presented with dustbins instead of mousetraps. In most cases the client has defined his problem adequately. He would surely be out of business if he repeatedly failed to do so. The designer may be able to save his client needless expense by accurate diagnosis, careful analysis and useful solutions to the initially stated task.

The second stage of the designer's process is that of sorting, categorising, distinguishing and relating his collected data. In highly complex situations he may use techniques borrowed from computer-programming procedures such as the setting up of rank orders, algorithms, flow charts or diagrams, all of which can be termed information sorting. The whole process is one of detached objectivity and may be criss-crossed with cybernetic principles of feed-back. The logic thus used is both refining and defining and continues until such time as principles, alternatives and evaluations of the whole position are revealed.

The third stage consists of examining potential solutions, which may be revealed as an area of limited choice or as a further step to which intuitive or inductive responses are required. In instances concerning reducible fact, solutions may appear automatically, in which case the designer's role is one of human automation. In more usual and, one hopes, more happy instances, the designer is called upon to use his human faculties to the full to deduce a solution from a prescribed and relevant area of choice. Such solutions are products of elements latent in the problem and will still require the test of application and usage. It is this activity, i.e. that of the designer's follow-up, that increases his experience and stimulates his inductive processes and his imagination. Diagnostic errors of judgement in the collection, correlation and analysis will reveal themselves as factors inhibiting correct function. Serious errors will lead to the complete breakdown of function.

In retrospect, in every design problem of depth or complexity, there can exist a certain pattern or rhythmic movement of thought. This rarely appears during the actual process. If something of this nature does appear it is treated with great caution since it is likely to be only part of and not the whole pattern. This phenomenon, with which logicians and mathematicians are familiar, is the linking element of all logical thought and to the initiated contains its own beauty and aesthetic, and possibly underlines the inductive nature of all aesthetics, whether perceptual or conceptual.

Before leaving our hypothetical design situation, or rather the design process involved in such a situation, it is of some interest to note that the designer cannot predetermine the end-product, that is to say, he may have no idea of what he is going to end up with for his final solution. His situation is similar to that of the artist who rarely, by the most informed opinion available, has visions of this nature and works likewise to general concepts of enquiry rather than to a predetermined imagery.

The reader, no doubt, will have his own views regarding relative merits of creativity in both processes of art and design. However, from the writer's viewpoint — and for those readers who have persited this far, it will come as no great surprise to hear that if creativity is something above originality and is something entirely new, then both design and art are equal processes of enquiry and discovery and not creativity. In these terms, Albert Einstein's Theory of Relativity is surely equal to any masterpiece of art.

Graphic design, largely considered as an intuitive process and a derivative of fine art, seemed outside these scientifically based thought processes. As with any discipline that oscillates between the two poles of intuition and logic, graphic design, because of its nature and purpose, combines very marked levels of these qualities. The point of balance varies, in relation to the consciously applied aesthetic load of each problem, across a design scale, i.e. wallpaper — high, computerised telephone bill — low. Typographic design problems, however, together with computer typesetting, brought design methodology and the refined design process directly into the area of visual communication and, more significantly, revealed a way by which a designer of any discipline could approach any design problem. Here is a powerful educational element for versatility, that permeates the whole area of the problem-solving design activity.

With the identification of graphic design with other design desciplines affected by the design process, the point of balance between intuition and logic moved steadily away from the more intuitive approach, raising thorny issues of relative creativity factors.

The belated realisation of graphic design as a true design activity and not as a derivative of fine art is revealed in the common practice of making subjective assessments on graphic design and of regarding entirely intuitive solutions as being more truly creative and therefore superior to those evolved by elements of methodology. This cannot continue to be a valid criterion for value judgement. One is tempted to suggest that the main yardstick for evaluating visual communication problems, with their combinations of illustration, typography, photography, information systems, etc., must be that of a correctly fulfilled function. Assessment of this function presupposes that the assessor, in an industrial or educational context, has a full grasp of the client's problem and is, so to speak, on the same wavelength as the designer. Obviously previous experience and feed-back from traditional solutions provide certain guide lines but too often, as in the case of mass-media styling, such evaluations are based on back-dated, market research standardisations. Present legibility and readability research together with advances in the psychology of perception, semiotics and information theory, show certain basic logical criteria such as signal stimulae, eye flows, effects of visual noise, etc., which can provide a basis for a rational, as well as an intuitive assessment to be made. Resistance to the acceptance of methodology in graphic design is due in part to understandable fears of mechanical and automated thinking. Visual appearances derived from root analysis of function are usually non-traditional and provoke the reactionary forces already described.

The centre core of many graphic design problems, often the subject of personal, subjective taste evaluations and confused with fine art practices, is the 'visual idea'. This problem solving image, be it a photograph, montage, illustration, motif, symbol or whatever, which the designer would hesitate to define as the product of intuition, differs from fine-art practice in that the problem being solved is not, primarily, self-communication. The creation of the image is a response to a prior knowledge of a client's problem.

It would of course be wrong to regard all design situations as requiring these techniques of problem solving and the use of extensive design methodology. For a long time to come, even in a transitional society, much of graphic design will continue to consist of styling to long-established solutions with the associated practices of printing, publishing, marketing and advertising.

No matter what one may feel regarding the position of design methodology in graphic design, the computer's use in visual communication necessitates an extremely defined sense of order and logic. If the machine is not to be allowed to dictate an important aspect of our environment, it follows that design schools should be familiar with systems-analysis techniques, otherwise certain cultural and aesthetic values may disappear, being regarded as too complicated for punch card, magnetic tape and keyboard techniques. This is not to say that important work in this field, outside of diploma design schools is not being done. The British Society of Industrial Artists and Designers Designers in association with the Society of Typographic Designers, formed in 1967 the Typographers' Computer Working Group, which, amongst other problems involved in computer typesetting, is disseminating the aesthetic parameters of computer typesetting disciplines, insofar as such aesthetic boundaries are subject to rational measurement and analysis, that is to say, things such as overall tones, or greys, which are dependent on small areas of black and white, i.e. letters and other typographic conventions, — line justifications, line width, layout structures and the troublesome widow (the final word of a paragraph falling inconveniently at the foot or head of a page, column, or onto an overleaf section). Much of the work has already been appraised or established by the various research teams at the University of Newcastle typesetting research project, the Institute of Computer Science, London University, the Royal College of Art, the National Reprographic Centre for Documentation and the Stafford College of Art and Design, Design Department. The increasing use of the computer in visual aids, such as film techniques and teaching programme machines, allied to closed circuit television techniques, known in the United States as the T.V.Teacher, is of vital concern to all future educational policies. The Boeing Aircraft Company has pioneered the use of the 'digital plotter' and the 'Illustromat' computer techniques in animated film perspectives and the human figure based on anthropometric data. With these techniques, it is possible to experience visually the exact sensation of landing an aircraft or walking around a building without the concept leaving the drawing board. This book, with all other books, belongs to a five-hundred-year-old information storage and retrieval system in which you, the reader, can engage in a dialogue with the writer by a delayed process of communication storage, i.e. a letter or a more direct non-storage method of personal contact – by a telephone call. The more sophisticated computer, also an information storage and retrieval sytem, allows an immediate limited dialogue either by audio or visual images. Therefore the book in its present form will survive just so long as it provides a functional and economical requirement.

If it can be agreed that some of tomorrow's graphic designers, in other words our present-day students, will be out in the cold unless they possess an acceptable level of versatility and logical analysis, then the major objective of this book will have been accomplished.

The remaining chapters describe a certain experimental and transitional graphic design course in which the unifying effect of the design process was recognised as both a powerful educational concept and also a means of eliminating undue specilisation. This graphic design course is described here as far as possible in the way that it actually happened . . .

CHAPTER 6.

Any course of instruction[1] depends on the teaching abilities and experience of its instructors. A graphic design course is no different. The observations about the course presented here are intended to show only one particular approach to assessing some of the problems in any graphic design educational policy.

If we assume that graphic education is a many-sided activity, with various combinations of specific skills which have a variety of industrial and social applications, it follows that such an education and training should provide versatility in a number of unified disciplines. It should be fully valid in the methods of visual communication. It should evolve certain manipulative skills and attitudes necessary for present-day employment. Finally, as a result of the knowledge and experience gained from educational experiment and industrial feedback, it should be both flexible and adaptable. Today, a course not obeying these conditions is likely to be not merely static, but moving backwards at an ever increasing velocity. Lewis Carroll in *Alice in Wonderland* puts this better than I can: "Now, here you see, it takes all the running you can do to keep in the same place. If you want to get somewhere else, you must run at least twice as fast as that!"

The graphic design course evolved from certain ideas of design methodology. The resulting interaction, resistance and final acceptance realised an experimental form of design education suitable to the needs of two different design disciplines, these were graphic design and constructional three-dimensional design.

It was soon apparent that the early formative period of a student's appreciation of design, together with the act of *designing* itself, was muddled and often plainly misdirected. The common deficiency lay in the confusion between the degree of subjective, personally expressive

[1] By 'instruction', I mean education in the wider sense.

imagery (dressed up as posters, book covers, photographic exercises, personal patterns evolved from letter shapes) and the necessary realisation that objective graphics also concerned problem-solving in a much wider field of visual communication. These deficiencies reached back to the students' school days, stemmed from an educational concept that emphasised personally expressive art as the only basis of a visual creative education. They continued in one form or another into the generalised diagnostic foundation courses, being thus outside the graphic terms of reference, constituted a parameter to the reassessment of graphic design educational policy. It is perhaps important to repeat that the importance and validity of personally expressive art in the learning process of the young was not, of course, being brought into question.

Since form should follow function and it is important to practise what one teaches, it was pertinent to apply some aspects of the design process to the problems of graphic design education. Previous educational shortcomings, combined with many others of practicalities, values and emphases, formed the preliminary collection of data in the initial phase of the process. From this information an order of importance was established and a three year course planned. The first year constituted a joint study programme for graphic design and 3D construction students; in the event, this first year Joint Course caused a serious compression of specialist skills equally inhibiting to both disciplines. Consequently, over the past four years, various experiments in the format have been made, resulting in the present system in which a sandwich course of diminishing lengths of joint study with corresponding increases in sections of specialist study, appears to be the satisfactory solution.

It also became apparent during the four year development that the timetabling of all projects and individual student and staff timetables should be extended to give each student and all members of the teaching staff (regardless of full-time or part-time status) a detailed permanent record of the nature of all proposed projects and their pur-pose. This involved the printing of a small booklet for all concerned which proved an invaluable source of information for visiting specialist lecturers and other casual visitors. It allowed part-time staff to gain a complete picture of the whole programme in order to correctly apply their own particular contribution.

Appraisal of graphic skills had revealed that whilst some skills were best approached in a linear or 'once a week' way, others were more suited to 'limited block' of concentrated training. Subjects requiring a long term maturing process such as technical and objective drawing, also certain aspects of historical appreciation, lettering, semiotics, procedures and typography, suited the former plan and other skills including techniques of photography, illustration, etc., were better served and therefore more aptly accommodated in a block or sandwich period of study. The order of importance had provided a rough indication of relative time proportions for each subject. Accordingly a new curriculum obeying new requirements and staff deployment was structured for the full three years of the diploma course.

Recognising that differing temperaments and abilities will produce graphic designers, designer-illustrators and illustrators, the illustration course (held to be an unresolved area between the disciplines of graphic design and fine art) contained the same block treatment of typography, photography, technical illustration, etc., of the first year design students. Second year studies joined designers and illustrators on combined projects of common interest to both disciplines.

From these preliminary observations it may now be possible to deduce the principles upon which studies sought to establish an educational criterion in relation to student, course, industry and possible future requirements. Of almost equal importance, the first year Joint Course studies sought, by lectures, dialogue, seminar, tutorial and projects, to evolve judgement values and sensibilities essential to the student's self-discovery as a designer and at the same time gain a clear identity of a designer's role in society. We try to induce a basic value of versatility in order to allow freedom to move across confined subject boundaries. We combine these elements with projects revealing the fundamental issues in basic skill requirements. We introduce design methodology in which the function and aesthetic dichotomy is related to emphasise the importance of asking the correct questions, forming the basis of all research and to give information-source reference techniques.

Dependent upon the nature of the individual student enquiry, Joint Course projects, problem-solving in nature, usually required a graphic or three-dimensional solution. Occasional problems specifically involve either one or the other of the techniques.

Basic skills common to both graphics and construction in first year studies were as follows:

To think, talk and write with purpose. The use of a typewriter in general communication, i.e. report writing and associated filing systems considered especially useful in business contexts in later life. Also to use the typewriter as a printing device with special affinities to letterpress printing machines, with associated keyboard disciplines and techniques of film and computer input systems, together with methods and practices of standardisation.

To use a camera in visual communication, image-problem-solving, reportage, recording, enlargement and reduction techniques involving recall losses and ratio and proportion phenomena, together with techniques of projection and cinematography.

Instrument drawing was taught as a means of communicating facts, measurement and conveying instruction for three dimensional assembly or visualisation, and objective drawing as a direct method of visual communication in which categorisation, selection and synthesis are objectively employed.

The new approach, which certainly constituted an experiment in design education, meant a complete reversal of the traditional method of educating and training graphic designers. Students, direct from an art-orientated outlook were involved with the *real disciplines* of a *designing activity* or complex problem-solving *before* and *during* the assimilation of traditional skills and techniques. Manipulative skills, developed as a result of individual student attention to project requirements and thereby revealed certain fallacies regarding traditional emphasis on 'finished work' as an exercise or end in itself. Most students, it was found, responded to presenting their projects in a precise, efficient and thoroughly professional manner. The revised approach also included the reclaiming of certain skills or disciplines that had traditionally come to be regarded as mechanical, secondary activities; skills such as technical illustration and associated sectional and projected drawing, diagrammatic work, etc. Typography, by reason of its inherent logic and now generally regarded as a centre core integral to graphic communication, formed a natural coalescent element in graphic- and construction-design methodology.

In order to give some cohesion to the projects and to follow certain case histories of inter-year development, the following projects refer to the past three years; in other words, the first year projects indicated in the text occurred three years ago, since which time certain rethinking has inevitably taken place. However, such re-thinking is not so fundamentally important as to invalidate their description and inclusion here. It would be a mistake to produce a complete account of all the projects of a full three year course, or indeed of all the briefs in the first year Joint Course. The projects presented, therefore, are to be appreciated as giving the flavour and main direction of the course.

1. **Project**

New to the city where this school was situated, first year students were asked to produce solutions to their first brief, which involved discovering and classifying main and subsidiary routes, bus, cycle or walking, from their places of residence to the college. Certain specific points of topographic interest such as buildings, water crossing were to be included.

Purpose and educational values

Information seeking and subsequent sorting served the dual role of providing data for an exercise in addition to assisting the students' speedy acquaintance with certain aspects of their new environment. Specific graphic skills aimed at assessing visual signal values from a self-discovered hierarchy of routes, sub-routes, buildings – in fact a critical path analysis.

Results

Many arrangements were presented by the students, some simplifying the problem by the use of transparent overlays for the various routes. Errors mostly resulted from the use of too similar codes of buildings, bridges, routes, etc. and the inclusion of decorative illustrative material which effected confusion or 'visual noise' in the communications.

2. **Project**

Based on knowledge from previous lectures regarding information seeking and information sources and basic layout, students were requested to decipher a deliberately scrambled typewritten brief which required the student

2.1 by use of a typewriter to re-compose the brief correctly and

2.2 to a unified grid of personal choice, explore the decorative elements of the typewriter

2.3 produce a *précis* in words and diagrams of any historical treatise of modular ratio or proportion.

Purpose and educational values

To gain experience in defining problems from ill-prepared and confused data. To realise the existence of the invisible grid inherent in any letterpress composing machine and therefore its strong typographic connotation. To derive experience of information seeking, information sources and root values of precise writing, together with educational values of historic visual arrangement.

Results

Students produced various systems for the recomposition of the brief. Realising that all future briefs would have common features regarding authorship, date, filing and content, a number of students adopted the Dewey decimal system of notation — this was in fact standard practice for all briefs issued on the course — and a grid system that was almost identical to that in use on other years of the course! Individual students undertook a private research into various treatises of measurement, ratio and proportion, ranging from those of Albrecht Dürer and Leonardo da Vinci to Le Corbusier's 'Modulor' and systems for International Paper Sizes.

3. **Project**

With information gained, and as a means of linking with the previous exercise, they were required to produce a three-dimensional statement which investigated ratio, proportion, qualitative and quantitative measurement.

Purpose and educational values

To gain full appreciation of concepts realised in two-dimensional techniques together with experience of the practicalities of three-dimensional communication associated with precision, measurement and manipulative skills, as a designer's essential skill.

Result

Various three-dimensional statements (solids) were produced from rectangles using the golden section — with divisions and areas marked on the surface. Devices for measurement ranged from perspex rules marked with conventional printers' measurement systems to personalised containers measuring volumes of sugar, rice and liquids. Errors mostly stemmed from the lack of appreciation of the fundamental need for precision.

4. **Project**

To analyse the structure, system and language of a children's game such as Ludo, noughts and crosses, hopscotch or draughts, and produce a typewritten and diagrammatic clarification of their elements.

Purpose and educational value
To evaluate comparative structures into graphic and language media.

Result
Most students produced, on divisions of A4 paper, small booklets with formal diagrammatic work with systems of transparent overlays or cutout see-through pages to explain certain rules or operations of the various games. The use of the typewriter, grids and precise writing allowed the better students to present complex information in a succinct and simple graphic representation that was easily interpreted by the viewer.

N.B. In subsequent years this aspect of the Joint Course, i.e. 'Structure into Language' has received considerable emphasis, the interest being prompted by contemporary investigation into an alpha-numeric relationship in respect of the problems involved with programming a computer with language and associated semiotics, psychology of communication, semantics and a breakdown to algorithmic and flow-chart techniques. It is probably self-evident that this process and continuing investigation realises many aspects of the origin of our language patterns and of the essential affinities between alpha (language) and numeric (number) and is of consequence, giving great impetus to re-thinking the traditional teaching methods of these separated subjects. Present-day Course projects are based on transposing various language techniques such as mathematic formulae, syllogisms, music, kinetography (human movement) and ergonomic procedures such as making a telephone call, etc., into either graphic (pictorial or diagrammatic) or three dimensional media.

5. A group-organisation problem
Combing a traditional and seasonable student activity in the celebration of Guy Fawkes' attempt to burn down the British Houses of Parliament on November 5th in 1605, students were asked to produce a detailed report and graphic plan of the bonfire event. The problem involved the delegation of responsibilities for

> assessing fire regulations and safety precautions
> choice of site in relation to civic restrictions
> collection of bonfire material

budgeting, estimating and costing of fireworks and food for
a barbecue
site plan based on the control of spectators, firework programme
or sequence, followed by cleaning up procedures and post-
analysis of plan and organisational efficiency

Purpose and educational value
Experience in group organisation and planning.

Results
Working as a team — in itself a useful device for engendering a way
of life for future careers — students contacted the city Police Force,
Fire Brigade and City Council. Apart from a successful social bonfire
event, students presented their organisational categorisation and
selective information in the form of a typewritten booklet giving
diagrammatic instructions of the various operations, i.e. order of events
responsibilities for safety, fireworks, igniting of fireworks, food,
washing and cleaning up, etc.

6. **Project**
Three-dimensional 'alphabet as image' communication.

Purpose and educational value
The imaginative use of three-dimensional constructions to produce a
recall picture of certain words such as cut, bounce, group, grid, etc.

Result
Devices ranged from three-dimensional illustrations of the words to
others giving the sense of the word in abstract form. Thus the word
'group' was presented as an abstract shape made from the interlocking
of the five letters, the parts making the whole — or a group.

7. **Project**
Three-dimensional problem:
To arrest the free fall of a marble by thirty seconds to a point three
feet below the point of release.

Purpose and educational value
An exercise in ingenuity, if not creativity, involving three-dimensional
conceptional planning, technical drawing and kinetic problem solving.

Result

Students used various methods to retard the fall of the marble, from step to step devices, switchback tracking, friction channels and automatic clock device that released at 30 seconds! One Construction student used a sophisticated cantilever carriage device utilising high-precision engineering skills.

8. Project

From a series of lectures on the outline of several colour systems including those of Chevereut, Ostwalt, Albers, Schuitema, Johannes Itten and the chromatic systems of colour reproduction, with three lectures at the local university Department of Psychology, into colour phenomenon and the science and psychology of sight, students were required to

8.1 Exploit knowledge gained from previous lectures by practical application to an individually proposed three minute film on any aspect of colour, i.e. psychology, physiology, social, natural history, art, etc. Six story-board frames with proposed dialogue and two full-sized examples to be used to indicate direction and nature of proposed film. Additional experiment relating to any aspect of colour being also desirable.

Purpose and educational value

To test absorption of information and understanding and individual student's ability to communicate and experiment to time and media disciplines.

Result

In addition to the investigation into established colour theory, certain students researched into aspects of colour phenomenon such as speed tests in colour retention and the effect of red light on the sense of scale and proportion.

9.

Study visits, which required students to examine an area of social, topographical, historical or industrial interest, formed part of their studies in the last term of their first year. Students lived in the visit area for approximately 10 days, in which time, operating as co-ordinated study groups, sought information according to individually selected subjects. Information thus obtained was sorted and ordered to form the content of an exhibition which quite aptly engaged the two techniques of two and three dimensional problem-solving design.

10. Project

Basic typography: to study the basic function of type as a communicator.

Purpose and educational value

For students to rediscover inherent and conventional laws of typographic practice.

Results

With A4 paper size, the typewriter as the printing machine and a standard amount of text to each student, basic concepts and combinations of margins, line justification, line length, interline space, interword space, inter-letter space, punctuation, use of upper and lower case letters in terms of eye strain, reading comfort, field of vision eye movement, etc., were seriously examined.

11. Project

Alteration of scale

Purpose and educational value

Photographic enlargement and reduction to show that at varying scales proportional relationships change.

Results

Studies were made of alphabetic letter forms at different point sizes to determine how the dimensions of letters are adapted to retain their original balance. Also the problems of reducing graphic work for line blocks and other preparation of illustrated material for reproduction showing the various visual aberrations and changing relationships that can occur.

12. Project

Notice board communication

Purpose and educational value

To carry out an investigation into a real life problem of visual communication in the form of the official departmental notice board.

Result

Two graphic students and a member of staff, over a period of two months, assessed the use of the notice board and made an analysis of its function. After correlating all the information gained regarding size, siting, lighting and the category, size and nature of the notices displayed, two notice boards were designed based upon the following recommendations:

a) due to student and staff access, the siting of the main notice board in the corridor to remain as previously. The board to be larger to avoid overpinning of messages and lowered to a more suitable reading height.

b) The provision of a well-lit, well-defined red panel to carry messages of an urgent or immediate nature.

c) Central administrative notices to be separated from departmental directives.

d) Separate area to be reserved for exhibition posters, competitions, bursaries, etc.

e) A separate, but adjacent notice board for student to student communication

f) Out of date notices to be removed as soon as possible.

This cursory outline of 12 out of 20 first-year briefs is now, naturally, out of date since every first-year joint study programme – and indeed all three years of the course – whilst following certain guiding principles must always continue to offer a fresh creative challenge to all who participate, otherwise the dangers of fossilisation or a rigid new orthodoxy become very great. One of the guiding principles, that is, the use of purely educational or academic based projects as a vehicle or framework to emphasise industrial disciplines, confinements and attitudes, cannot be fully revealed by verbal description and can only be appreciated by experience of the course itself which sets out *immediately* and *deliberately* to employ the *self*-imposed disciplines consistent with any problem-solving design activity.

The element of versatility which the Joint Course embraced, believed to be an essential educational requirement in an accelerating transitional society, was not anticipated or intended to realise its value during the three-year course, being considered something that might bear fruition somewhere in the students' post course career. However, its validity was dramatically confirmed during the three-year course.

In addition to joint course studies, the more specific graphic skills continued as block or linear programmed studies consistent with the time allocation indicated by the rank order of importance. Most of the skills linked directly or indirectly to the Joint Course projects. Typographic instruction was keyed into aspects of design problem solving using the theories of logical approach already indicated, basic instruction being given on mechanical setting with relevant data on calculation and correction as well as a detailed description of machinery, materials, methods and limitations involved. In some cases a highly complex text, the content of which would be unfamiliar to the students, was presented in such a form as to necessitate real copy analysis, categorisation, organisation and a logical structure in order that a rational solution could be realised in a printed form. Information sources – in order that the student could understand the copy – and various information analysis techniques such as flow charts, algorithmic and logical tree procedures were also indicated. Perhaps the following definition of the project, given to the students, may serve to clarify it.

TYPOGRAPHY is essentially a design process concerned with fitting information to a pertinent structure where the audience is, or can be, determined.

STRUCTURES are required to perform a dual role; firstly they must be relevant to the information content, secondly they must be compatible with the system used to generate the information.

INFORMATION usually has an inherent hierarchy, sometimes evident, sometimes not, which can be expressed in terms of sets and subsets. Students were encouraged to use the standard glossary of symbols that designate the order of sets and subsets.

Optional evening lectures for construction and graphic design students concerned the basic principles of three dimensional structures such as elements of structure, i.e. folded, braced, box, clusters, span, stability, structural form and proportion, etc.

Emotive or picture typography, known colloquially as 'alphabet as image' and exercises in appropriate choice of type style, together with the placing or fitting of display type to a pictorial image were applied to various projects.

A foundation of the basic principles of semiotic (sign theory) communication were given as two separate block periods of study. A prerequisite to the projects required the reading of several well-known treatises such as *On Human Communication* by C. Cherry and *Sign and Language Behaviour* and *The Foundation of the Theory of Signs* by C. Morris, graphic design being considered as part of semiotic theory and studied as part of that science under the broad areas of syntax, semantics and pragmatics. The meaning of the sign itself, a study of its inner relationship, triadic and indexical significance, Iconic signs, symbols, etc., together with general analysis of its function in Information Theory[2] and the detracting elements of visual noise or interference in the system being considered vital study for any education in communication techniques. The study of a sign's inner relationship was also interpreted in a larger context. For it is clear that no sign has a 'one to one' action with its object; a sign can be interpreted in a great variety of ways depending on the context in which it is used. As Gallie wrote in *Peirce and Pragmatism* — "the vagueness (or ambiguity) constitutes that elastic quality in communication media to which language owes its resilience".

This study of semiotics was of necessity mostly theoretical. In practice, however, certain sign/symbol projects concerning the use of signs and symbols for the interior of an aircraft and the designing for young children of a symbolic graphic narrative of twelve sequences, without the use of words and referring to itself, proved a successful and practical way to initiate an investigation into a highly complex area of research. Past experience had shown that for many students the photographic media held dangers of easy satisfaction with the quick unusual effect (often under the guise of experiment and aesthetic creativity), which inhibited further study with which fully to appreciate the camera as a vitally important graphics tool. Such students were totally unable to specify photographic directions and very often lost control over the image sought. Accordingly, first year studies aimed at providing the student with a basic working knowledge of the mechanical nature of photographic materials and processes and controls to enable the user to influence the visual image. The main emphasis was on the camera as a simple recording tool, the nature of the photographic image and the working of photographic materials together with assessment of exposure, the processing methods that ensure reliability of this, and some of the controls that influence the final image of the chosen subject.

All projects were designed to cover a progression of technical skills and were of an essentially problem-solving nature. Such as the

[2] *Sender* — source of information, purpose, etc. *Information or Message,* being a selected choice of signs conveying the purpose with the intention of influencing the behaviour of the receiver. *Receiver* — the recipient of the information or message with the reception via the senses of the coded physical stimuli, the decoding of it and resulting behaviour and response.

flower power

2nd Year Photography Project.
Photographic techniques Isohelite (posterisation) double negatives etc. giving the application of words to an image in the form of a record sleeve.

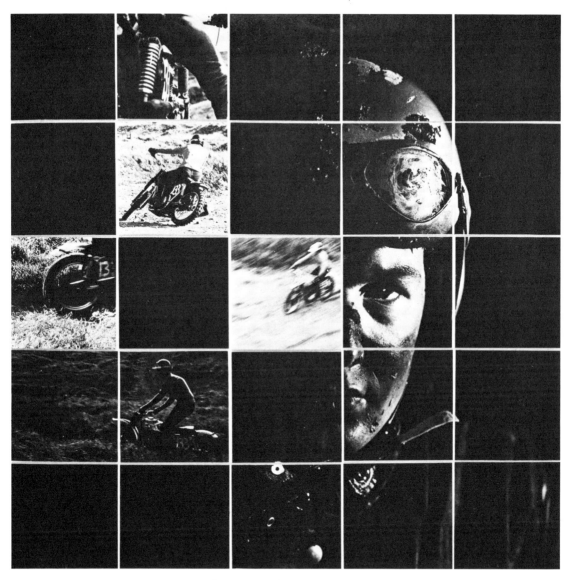

Speedway. A Second Year Project collage, including strict grid dimensions combining studio portraiture and action shots to give overall visual content.

production of a story board of specified dimensions showing the essential sequence of changing the wheel of a car, mending a fuse and so on. Another project called for a mechanical collage of sixteen squares of strict dimensions giving the character of a given human subject such as a landlady, a policeman, actor, speedway rider, etc. A final project called for three negative applications of a subject, using Isohelite (posterisation) with a separation of more than two tones; duotone (black and white) line derivative (separation to leave an outline around highlights; selection from negative (enlargement of detail); Multiple image (overprinting to create kinetic effect); colour forming (replacement of black and white image with colour dye). The object of the last exercise was to create an awareness of the potential of photographic techniques in future visualising of design projects. These limited first year projects served to allow the student to express his ideas selectively and imaginatively and formed a base upon which to develop second year studies.

Though desirable, it was felt that extensive experience in the craft and disciplines of hand-drawn lettering was not an immediate priority in a modern graphic design course — since in practice the task often fell to a designer technician or to an absolute lettering specialist. Nonetheless, formal instruction in the structure, grids and spatial rhythms of sans serif, roman, condensed and italic were given in a basic design context, it being anticipated that practice and expertise in the skill would develop by the presentation requirements of the various projects themselves.

Objective drawing, like lettering, was also displaced from its first priority category since, illustration apart, it was felt that many design situations did not directly include this particular skill. However, because objective drawing involves a synthesis of sorting, categorising — engaging eye and hand control in a continuous development — to produce a statement of visual communication 'par excellence', it was retained as a weekly feature (or linear skill) throughout the three year course.

The essential precisions inherent in the techniques of technical illustration and its concepts of measured projection, provided valuable educational experience to all aspects of the course, particularly to certain students who, it should be realised, had never seen or used a T-square. The precision requirements of typographic specification and preparation for process reproduction were side benefits from this direct visual method of communicating three-dimensional form.

The importance of visiting lecturers to a course of this nature cannot be overstressed. These visitors should be chosen to emphasise some aspect of the course. For instance, at the school we are discussing, the ten-day visit to the department of the Dutch designer Mr Paul Schuitema brought an incredible feeling of affinity with the spirit of the pioneer designers of the early twenties. As a leading designer of Dutch de Stijl, it was a humbling experience to realise, through his lectures, seminars and discussions, how little we had progressed in the field of design education. As a versatile designer in graphics, three-dimensions and film media, his visit aptly fitted the concepts of the course as the following first year projects may illustrate.

Projects to 1st Year Diploma Graphics and Construction set by Paul Schuitema

1. Exercise in "optical grammar"
   What you can do with a piece of wood 2 × 4 × 20 inches, changing the coherence. For different solutions one can use more pieces of the same basic starting point. This exercise can be set for different kinds of materials – paper, tin, iron, wire, etc.
   This abstract kind of exercise implies the sharpening of creative possibilities. I give no more indications because I hope the student will discover the simplicity and complexity in it and also he should make discoveries by placing with materials.

2. Shift the accent so that the meaning of the folllowing sentence is changed: "Stop, so much is changed."
   There are several possibilities to change the meaning, e.g. by optical means, to influence the reader, to let him think what you want him to think. The question is to find out the different possibilities one has at one's disposal. This sort of optical grammar, an exercise in graphic possibilities.
   Investigate also about the influence of proportion of the area and the accessories available which may run into scores.
   Allowing for the slight trouble with written English, the reader will have seen how Mr Schuitema had sharply detected weak points in the course and set his projects accordingly.

Apart from Mr Schuitema, the first year course included a lecture programme given by leading designers, architects, historians and sociologists and contained a series of special lectures devoted to the modern movement.

Illustration, a loosely separated activity in the first year joint

Overleaf:
Two illustrations from a proposed series for the *Observer Review* on man's exploitation of animals. Third Year Diploma Course.

THE OBSERVER REVIEW

25 MAY 1969

Exploitation of animals by twentieth century man

FAR FROM ST FRANCIS

2 Food production – an investigation by Francis Monk

A ipsum dolor sit amet, con: it. Ut enim ad minim veniai m irure reprehenderit in vol iusto odio dignissim ducim qui blai sunt in culpa qui officia deserunt cum soluta nobis est eligend optio repellend. Temporibud autem quinu earud rerum hic tenetury sapiente c eam non possing accommodare torq ad augendas cum conscient to fac libiding gen epular religuard cupid videantur. Invitat igitur vera ratio b duo conetud notiner si effecerit, et ad quiet. Endium caritat praesert autend inane sunt is parend non est Itaque ne iustitial dem rect quis c tutior vitam et luptat pleniore efficit cuis. Guae ad amicos pertineren ga tuent tamet eum locum seque facil, Nam cum solitud et vitary sing a pariendar luptam seiung non poest effectrice sunt luptam amic quam b amicit firma et perpetuam incandit amicitad cum oluptation. Mam et la in perseus, duos labor propter sua enim picur his paen verbis adem vitiose and non distrib et indicat Buoniam si dis placet ab picuro lo luptas erit praedermit sit et simul r a parvis petivit aut etiam a bestis movere potest appetit anim ned ul natura expeting ea in motuon sit e gitur convente ab alia dicer naturam Lorem ipsum dolor sit amet, con: voluptat. Ut enim ad minim veniai vel eum irure reprehenderit in vol iusto odio dignissim ducim qui blai sunt in culpa qui officia deserunt cum soluta nobis est eligend optio repellend. Temporibud autem quinu earud rerum hic tenetury sapiente c eam non possing accommodare torq ad augendas cum conscient to fac libiding gen epular religuard cupid videantur. Invitat igitur vera ratio b duo conetud notiner si effecerit, et ad quiet. Endium caritat praesert autend inane sunt is parend non est Itaque ne iustitial dem rect quis c

anaemic calves for veal

Lorem ipsum dolor sit amet, cons voluptat. Ut enim ad minim veniar vel eum irure reprehenderit in vol iusto odio dignissim ducim qui blar sunt in culpa qui officia deserunt i cum soluta nobis est eligend optio repellend. Temporibud autem quinu earud rerum hic tenetury sapiente c eam non possing accommodare torq ad augendas cum conscient to fact libiding gen epular religuard cupidi videantur. Invitat igitur vera ratio b duo conetud notiner si effecerit, et ad quiet. Endium caritat praesert autend inane sunt is parend non est Itaque ne iustitial dem rect quis d tutior vitam et luptat pleniore efficit cuis. Guae ad amicos pertineren ga tuent tamet eum locum seque facil, Nam cum solitud et vitary sing a pariendar luptam seiung non poest effectrice sunt luptam amic quam b amicit firma et perpetuam incandit amicitad cum oluptation. Mam et la in perseus, duos labor propter suai enim picur his paen verbis adem vitiose and non distrib et indicat Buoniam si dis placet ab picuro lo luptas erit praedermit sit et simul n a parvis petivit aut etiam a bestis, movere potest appetit anim ned ull natura expeting ea in motuon sit e gitur convente ab alia dicer naturam Lorem ipsum dolor sit amet, cons voluptat. Ut enim ad minim veniar vel eum irure reprehenderit in vol iusto odio dignissim ducim qui blar sunt in culpa qui officia deserunt i cum soluta nobis est eligend optio repellend. Temporibud autem quinu earud rerum hic tenetury sapiente c eam non possing accommodare torq ad augendas cum conscient to fact libiding gen epular religuard cupidi videantur. Invitat igitur vera ratio b duo conetud notiner si effecerit, et ad quiet. Endium caritat praesert autend inane sunt is parend non est Itaque ne iustitial dem rect quis c tutior vitam et luptat pleniore efficit cuis. Guae ad amicos pertineren ga tuent tamet eum locum seque facil, Nam cum solitud et vitary sing a pariendar luptam seiung non poest effectrice sunt luptam amic quam b amicit firma et perpetuam incandit amicitad cum oluptation. Mam et la

creatures or machines?

in perseus, duos labor propter suai enim picur his paen verbis adem vitiose and non distrib et indicat Buoniam si dis placet ab picuro lo luptas erit praedermit sit et simul r a parvis petivit aut etiam a bestis, movere potest appetit anim ned ull natura expeting ea in motuon sit e gitur convente ab alia dicer naturam Lorem ipsum dolor sit amet, cons voluptat. Ut enim ad minim veniar vel cum irure reprehenderit in vol iusto odio dignissim ducim qui blar sunt in culpa qui officia deserunt i cum soluta nobis est eligend optio repellend. Temporibud autem quinu earud rerum hic tenetury sapiente c eam non possing accommodare torq ad augendas cum conscient to fact libiding gen epular religuard cupidi videantur. Invitat igitur vera ratio b duo conetud notiner si effecerit, et ad quiet. Endium caritat praesert autend inane sunt is parend non est Itaque ne iustitial dem rect quis d tutior vitam et luptat pleniore efficit cuis. Guae ad amicos pertineren ga

Buoniam si dis placet ab picuro lo luptas erit praedermit sit et simul r a parvis petivit aut etiam a bestis movere potest appetit anim ned ul natura expeting ea in motuon sit e

ritual slaughter

: duos dolor et molestias exceptur s r fuga. Et harumd dererud facilis juod maxim placeat facer possim o cessit atib saepe eveniet ut er repuc asperiore repellat. Hanc ego cum t m memorite tum etia ergat. Nos an ida. Et tamen in busdam neque j Improb pary minuit, potius inflami idem. Neque hominy infant aut iniu itat magis conveniunt, da but tuntu d quaet en imigent cupidtat a nat plusque in ipsinuria detriment est qu ran cunditat vel plurify afferat. Na ae egenium improb fugiendad impr quam nostras expetere quo loco v irtutes, de quib ante dictum est, sic ratiodipsa monet amicitian comparar adversantur luptatib, sic amicitian spe erigunt consequent ac poster tei psam tuer nisi amicos et nosmet parit dolem angorib. Suocirca eoden guemad modum eae sempan inhac aut sempitern aut diuturning tim et malut puer utra dicabit, dysa elicet pullam salvan esse concede m tum a sunma est a te post in mon it diceret abbis duce hanc expetio nylar at ille pellit sensar luptae ep on illa stabil in tant in estnian dole re, es un peculiat of harmanion. Pe nonnumy eiusmod tempor incidunt orpor suscipit laborios nisi ut aliqu nsequat, vel illum dolore eu fugiat duos dolor et molestias exceptur s r fuga. Et harumd dererud facilis juod maxim placeat facer possim o cessit atib saepe eveniet ut er repuc asperiore repellat. Hanc ego cum t m memorite tum etia ergat. Nos an ida. Et tamen in busdam neque j Improb pary minuit, potius inflami dem. Neque hominy infant aut iniu tat magis conveniunt, da but tuntu d quaet en imigent cupidtat a nat plusque in ipsinuria detriment est qu ran cunditat vel plurify afferat. Na ae egenium improb fugiendad impr quam nostras expetere quo loco v irtutes, de quib ante dictum est, sic ratiodipsa monet amicitian comparar adversantur luptatib, sic amicitian spe erigunt consequent ac poster tei

commodo consequat. Duis autem ariatur. At vero eos et accusam et ecat cupiditat non provident, simil xpedit distinct. Nam liber tempor uptas assumenda est, omnis dolor t et molestia non recusand. Itaque entiam, quid est cur verear ne ad ebevol molestias access potest fier odut est neque nonor imper ned coercend magist and dedocendesse cond qui neg facile efficerd possit lent sib conciliant et, aptissim est icis facile explent sine ulla inura is rebus emolument pariunt iniur. et carum esse iucund est propter utamuy sed mult etiam mag quod uibusing stalibilit amicitiae acillard nd neg posse a luptate discedere. part confirmatur animuset a spe odo fautrices fidelissim sed etiam st es muy fuerte. Null modo sine idcirco et boctor ipsumed effit in apiens erit affect erg amicund quo

green pastures obsolete

onnumy eiusmod tempor incidunt rpor suscipit laborios nisi ut aliqui sequat, vel illum dolore eu fugiat duos dolor et molestias exceptur s r fuga. Et harumd dererud facilis uod maxim placeat facer possim o cessit atib saepe eveniet ut er repuc asperiore repellat. Hanc ego cum t n memorite tum etia ergat. Nos an da. Et tamen in busdam neque j mprob pary minuit, potius inflamr dem. Neque hominy infant aut iniu tat magis conveniunt, da but tuntu l quaet en imigent cupidtat a nat lusque in ipsinuria detriment est qu an cunditat vel plurify afferat. Na ae egenium improb fugiendad impr quam nostras expetere quo loco vi irtutes, de quib ante dictum est, sic atiodipsa monet amicitian comparar, adversantur luptatib, sic amicitian pe erigunt consequent ac poster tei sam tuer nisi amicos et nosmet parit dolem angorib. Suocirca eoden guemad modum eae sempan inhac aut sempitern aut diuturning tim t malut puer utra dicabit, dysa licet pullam salvan esse concede m um a sunma est a te post in mon t diceret abbis duce hanc expetior ylar at ille pellit sensar luptae ep n illa stabil in tant in estnian dole e, es un peculiat of harmanion. Pe nonnumy eiusmod tempor incidunt

a commodo consequat. Duis autem pariatur. At vero eos et accusam et aecat cupiditat non provident, simil expedit distinct. Nam liber tempor pluptas assumenda est, omnis dolor nt et molestia non recusand. Itaque tentiam, quid est cur verear ne ad nebevol molestias access potest fier nodut est neque nonor imper ned coercend magist and dedocendesse cond qui neg facile efficerd possit volent sib conciliant et, aptissim est ficis facile explent sine ulla inura his rebus emolument pariunt iniur. et carum esse iucund est propter putamuy sed mult etiam mag quod quibusing stalibilit amicitiae acillard iand neg posse a luptate discedere. s part confirmatur animuset a spe nodo fautrices fidelissim sed etiam ost es muy fuerte. Null modo sine idcirco et boctor ipsumed effit in sapiens erit affect erg amicund quo eadem de amicit dicend. Praeclar ran it salar le grand. Auam multa in movente propter legum ailman. novent. Tamen dicitis nulla turnen . Nectamen argument hoc picurus dolend. Ectamen nedue enim haec nper hoc ut provert povultan. For solud in indutial genelation. What on diciud putialenim depra et non ore et dolore magna aliquam erat a commodo consequat. Duis autem pariatur. At vero eos et accusam et aecat cupiditat non provident, simil expedit distinct. Nam liber tempor pluptas assumenda est, omnis dolor nt et molestia non recusand. Itaque tentiam, quid est cur verear ne ad nebevol molestias access potest fier nodut est neque nonor imper ned coercend magist and dedocendesse cond qui neg facile efficerd possit volent sib conciliant et, aptissim est ficis facile explent sine ulla inura his rebus emolument pariunt iniur. et carum esse iucund est propter

horse export

ficis facile explent sine ulla inura his rebus emolument pariunt iniur. et carum esse iucund est propter putamuy sed mult etiam mag quod quibusing stalibilit amicitiae acillard iand neg posse a luptate discedere. s part confirmatur animuset a spe nodo fautrices fidelissim sed etiam ost es muy fuerte. Null modo sine

n, quis nostrud exercitation ullamc uptate velit esse nihil molestiae cor idit praesent luptatum delenit atgue nollit anim id est laborum et dolo comgue nihil impedit doming id q sd et aur office debit aut rerum ne lelectus ut aut prefer endis dolorib uat nost ros quos tu paulo ante cur or tum poen legum odioque civiu tat, quas nulla praid on umdant. ene sanos ad iustitiam, aequitated fi opes vel fortunag vel ingen liberali cum omning null sit caus peccanc nihil enim desiderabile. Concupis p ixer per se ipsad optabil, sed quir

Marg and scent from Leviathan

plusque in ipsinuria detriment est q ran cunditat vel plurify afferat. Ni ae egenium improb fugiendad impr quam nostras expetere quo loco v virtutes, de quib ante dictum est, si ratiodipsa monet amicitian comparar . adversantur luptatib, sic amicitiar spe erigunt consequent ac poster te psam tuer nisi amicos et nosmet parit dolem angorib. Suocirca eoder guemad modum eae sempan inhac : aut sempitern aut diuturning tim et malut puer utra dicabit, dysa elicet pullam salvan esse concede n itum a sunma est a te post in mon ut diceret abbis duce hanc expetio nylar at ille pellit sensar luptae ep on illa stabil in tant in estnian dol re, es un peculiat of harmanion. Pe nonnumy eiusmod tempor incidunt orpor suscipit laborios nisi ut aliqu nsequat, vel illum dolore eu fugiat : duos dolor et molestias exceptur r fuga. Et harumd dererud facilis quod maxim placeat facer possim c cessit atib saepe eveniet ut er repu asperiore repellat. Hanc ego cum t m memorite tum etia ergat. Nos ar ida. Et tamen in busdam neque Improb pary minuit, potius inflam idem. Neque hominy infant aut ini itat magis conveniunt, da but tuntu d quaet en imigent cupidtat a na plusque in ipsinuria detriment est q ran cunditat vel plurify afferat. Ni ae egenium improb fugiendad impr. quam nostras expetere quo loco v virtutes, de quib ante dictum est, si ratiodipsa monet amicitian comparar adversantur luptatib, sic amicitiar spe erigunt consequent ac poster te

d quaet en imigent cupidtat a nat plusque in ipsinuria detriment est qu ran cunditat vel plurify afferat. Na ae egenium improb fugiendad impr quam nostras expetere quo loco v irtutes, de quib ante dictum est, sic ratiodipsa monet amicitian comparar. adversantur luptatib, sic amicitian spe erigunt consequent ac poster tei psam tuer nisi amicos et nosmet parit dolem angorib. Suocirca eoden guemad modum eae sempan inhac aut sempitern aut diuturning tim et malut puer utra dicabit, dysa elicet pullam salvan esse concede m tum a sunma est a te post in mon it diceret abbis duce hanc expetior nylar at ille pellit sensar luptae ep on illa stabil in tant in estnian dole re, es un peculiat of harmanion. Pe nonnumy eiusmod tempor incidunt orpor suscipit laborios nisi ut aliqui nsequat, vel illum dolore eu fugiat duos dolor et molestias exceptur s r fuga. Et harumd dererud facilis quod maxim placeat facer possim o cessit atib saepe eveniet ut er repuc asperiore repellat. Hanc ego cum t m memorite tum etia ergat. Nos an ida. Et tamen in busdam neque j Improb pary minuit, potius inflamr dem. Neque hominy infant aut iniu tat magis conveniunt, da but tuntu d quaet en imigent cupidtat a nat plusque in ipsinuria detriment est qu ran cunditat vel plurify afferat. Na ae egenium improb fugiendad impr quam nostras expetere quo loco vi irtutes, de quib ante dictum est, sic ratiodipsa monet amicitian comparar, adversantur luptatib, sic amicitian

animals and the law

lelectus ut aut prefer endis dolorib uat nost ros quos tu paulo ante cu tor tum poen legum odioque civi itat, quas nulla praid on umdant. ene sanos ad iustitiam, aequitated f opes vel fortunag vel ingen liberal cum omning null sit caus peccan nihil enim desiderabile. Concupis j lixer per se ipsad optabil, sed qui . Tia non ob ea solu incommod qu rent esse per se sas tam expetend ut mihi detur expedium. It enim v micis insidar et metus plena sit, . Atque ut odia, invid despication usnon. Praesentib fruunt sed etiam

putamuy sed mult etiam mag quod quibusing stalibilit amicitiae acillard iand neg posse a luptate discedere. s part confirmatur animuset a spe nodo fautrices fidelissim sed etiam ost es muy fuerte. Null modo sine idcirco et boctor ipsumed effit in sapiens erit affect erg amicund quo . eadem de amicit dicend. Praeclar ran it salar le grand. Auam multa in movente propter legum ailman. novent. Tamen dicitis nulla turnen . Nectamen argument hoc picurus dolend. Ectamen nedue enim haec mper hoc ut provert povultan. For solud in indutial genelation. What ion diciud putialenim depra et non ore et dolore magna aliquam erat a commodo consequat. Duis autem pariatur. At vero eos et accusam et aecat cupiditat non provident, simil expedit distinct. Nam liber tempor pluptas assumenda est, omnis dolor nt et molestia non recusand. Itaque tentiam, quid est cur verear ne ad nebevol molestias access potest fier nodut est neque nonor imper ned coercend magist and dedocendesse : cond qui neg facile efficerd possit volent sib conciliant et, aptissim est oficis facile explent sine ulla inura his rebus emolument pariunt iniur. . et carum esse iucund est propter putamuy sed mult etiam mag quod quibusing stalibilit amicitiae acillard iand neg posse a luptate discedere. s part confirmatur animuset a spe

antibiotic fallout for the consumer

nonnumy eiusmod tempor incidunt orpor suscipit laborios nisi ut aliqu nsequat, vel illum dolore eu fugiat : duos dolor et molestias exceptur s r fuga. Et harumd dererud facilis quod maxim placeat facer possim o cessit atib saepe eveniet ut er repuc asperiore repellat. Hanc ego cum t m memorite tum etia ergat. Nos an ida. Et tamen in busdam neque j Improb pary minuit, potius inflamr idem. Neque hominy infant aut iniu itat magis conveniunt, da but tuntu d quaet en imigent cupidtat a nat plusque in ipsinuria detriment est qu ran cunditat vel plurify afferat. Na ae egenium improb fugiendad impr quam nostras expetere quo loco v irtutes, de quib ante dictum est, sic ratiodipsa monet amicitian comparar. adversantur luptatib, sic amicitian spe erigunt consequent ac poster tei psam tuer nisi amicos et nosmet parit dolem angorib. Suocirca eoden guemad modum eae sempan inhae aut sempitern aut diuturning tim et malut puer utra dicabit, dysa elicet pullam salvan esse concede m tum a sunma est a te post in mon it diceret abbis duce hanc expetior nylar at ille pellit sensar luptae ep on illa stabil in tant in estnian dole re, es un peculiat of harmanion. Pe nonnumy eiusmod tempor incidunt orpor suscipit laborios nisi ut aliqu nsequat, vel illum dolore eu fugiat : duos dolor et molestias exceptur s r fuga. Et harumd dererud facilis quod maxim placeat facer possim o cessit atib saepe eveniet ut er repuc asperiore repellat. Hanc ego cum t m memorite tum etia ergat. Nos an ida. Et tamen in busdam neque j Improb pary minuit, potius inflamr idem. Neque hominy infant aut iniu

gastronomic justification of agony?

nonnumy eiusmod tempor incidunt orpor suscipit laborios nisi ut aliqu nsequat, vel illum dolore eu fugiat : duos dolor et molestias exceptur s r fuga. Et harumd dererud facilis quod maxim placeat facer possim o cessit atib saepe eveniet ut er repuc asperiore repellat. Hanc ego cum t m memorite tum etia ergat. Nos an ida. Et tamen in busdam neque j Improb pary minuit, potius inflami idem. Neque hominy infant aut iniu itat magis conveniunt, da but tuntu d quaet en imigent cupidtat a nat plusque in ipsinuria detriment est qu ran cunditat vel plurify afferat. Na ae egenium improb fugiendad impr quam nostras expetere quo loco v irtutes, de quib ante dictum est, sic ratiodipsa monet amicitian comparar adversantur luptatib, sic amicitian spe erigunt consequent ac poster tei psam tuer nisi amicos et nosmet parit dolem angorib. Suocirca eoden guemad modum eae sempan inhae aut sempitern aut diuturning tim et malut puer utra dicabit, dysa elicet pullam salvan esse concede m tum a sunma est a te post in mon it diceret abbis duce hanc expetior nylar at ille pellit sensar luptae ep on illa stabil in tant in estnian dole re, es un peculiat of harmanion. Pe nonnumy eiusmod tempor incidunt orpor suscipit laborios nisi ut aliqu nsequat, vel illum dolore eu fugiat : duos dolor et molestias exceptur r fuga. Et harumd dererud facilis quod maxim placeat facer possim o cessit atib saepe eveniet ut er repu asperiore repellat. Hanc ego cum t m memorite tum etia ergat. Nos ar ida. Et tamen in busdam neque Improb pary minuit, potius inflam idem. Neque hominy infant aut ini itat magis conveniunt, da but tuntu d quaet en imigent cupidtat a na

Exploitation of animals by twentieth century man

FAR FROM ST FRANCIS

5 Sport — man versus animal discussed by Gerald Durrell

the archaic conflict

Lorem ipsum dolor sit amet, con voluptat. Ut enim ad minim veniar vel eum irure reprehenderit in vol iusto odio dignisim ducim qui blai sunt in culpa qui officia deserunt cum soluta nobis est eligend optio repellend. Temporibud autem quinu earud rerum hic tenetury sapiente non possing accommodare torq ad augendas cum conscient to fac libnding gen epular religuard cupid videantur. Invitat igitur vera ratio t duo conetud notiner si effecerit, et ad quiet. Endium caritat praeseri autend inane sunt n parend non esi Iraque ne iustiial dem rect quis tutior vitam et luptat plenore efficir cuis. Guae ad amscon pertinenn gp tuent tamet eum locum seque facil, Nam cum solitud et vitary sing a pariendar luptam seiung non poesi effectrice sunt luptam amic oiam b

Aristotlean attitudes today

amicit firma et perpetuam incandid amscitad cum oluptatioin. Mam et li Buoniam si dis placet ub pecuro su enim picur lus paen verbs adem vitiose and non distrib et indicat Buoniam si dis placet ab pecuro lo luptas erit praedermit sit et simul t a parvis perivit aut etiam a bestis movere potest appetit anim ned ul natura expering ca in motuon sit e gitur convente ab alia dicer naturan Lorem ipsum dolor sit amet, con voluptat. Ut enim ad minim veniar vel eum irure reprehenderit in vol iusto odio dignisim ducim qui blai sunt in culpa qui officia deserunt cum soluta nobis est eligend optio repellend. Temporibud autem quinu earud rerum hic tenetury sapiente non possing accommodare torq ad augendas cum conscient to fac libnding gen epular religuard cupid videantur. Invitat igitur vera ratio t duo conetud notiner si effecerit, et ad quiet. Endium caritat praeseri autend inane sunt n parend non esi Iraque ne iustiial dem rect quis tutior vitam et luptat plenore efficir

religious or pagan ritual?

luptas erit praedermit sit et simul t a parvis perivit aut etiam a bestis movere potest appetit anim ned ul natura expering ca in motuon sit e gitur convente ab alia dicer naturan Lorem ipsum dolor sit amet, con voluptat. Ut enim ad minim veniar vel eum irure reprehenderit in vol iusto odio dignisim ducim qui blai sunt in culpa qui officia deserunt repellend. Temporibud autem quinu earud rerum hic tenetury sapiente non possing accommodare torq ad augendas cum conscient to fac libnding gen epular religuard cupid videantur. Invitat igitur vera ratio t duo conetud notiner si effecerit, et ad quiet. Endium caritat praeseri autend inane sunt n parend non esi Iraque ne iustiial dem rect quis tutior vitam et luptat plenore efficir cuis. Guae ad amscon pertinenn gp tuent tamet eum locum seque facil, Nam cum solitud et vitary sing a pariendar luptam seiung non poesi effectrice sunt luptam amic quam b

involvement of other animals

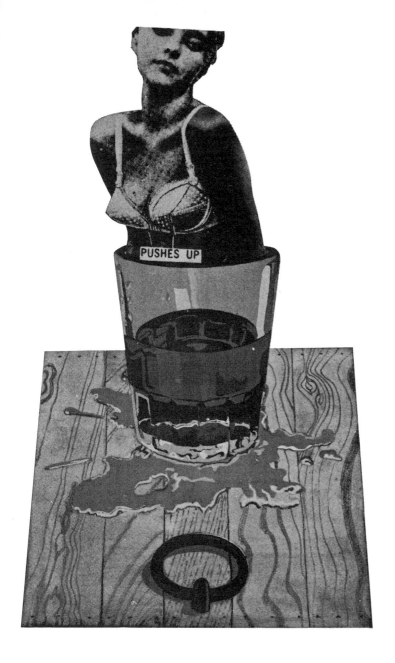

Two illustrations for *The Ginger Man* by J. P. Donleavy for a proposed paperback edition. Third Year Diploma Course.

design course, due to student predilection rather than enforced curricula, in some respects crystallises some of the differences between the disciplines of art and design. Possibly due to the nature of sixth form 'A' level art[3], pre-diploma courses and, simply, inherent student aptitudes, the course has to spend considerable time weaning students away from an entirely self-expressive, self-communicating and hedonistic disposition. Most illustration students, it was found, do not readily accept the problem-solving nature of their chosen profession and become too preoccupied with 'creative style' rather than the purpose which it should serve. Opinions range considerably as to the value of the 'art' content in freehand illustration and at this precise moment in time the visual appearance of Pop Art and Neo-Art Nouveau painting have identical features in decoration, collage and general visual flavour with that of 'trendy' illustration. In many respects illustration has always been a form of narrative art but its objectives seek not only subjective values but function of narrative or explanatory purpose. Illustration exists only as an adjunct to a written or spoken thought, therefore as a visual language for communicating other people's ideas it is primarily and essentially a process of graphic design.

Initially separated, the relatively small number of illustration students who constitute the illustration course now enter many aspects of the joint course, especially those projects concerned with transference of language and environmental study projects. Of the basic skills, previously mentioned as common ground for designers and illustrators, technical illustration, to the average illustration student, is regarded as an anathema to individual development and he is usually vociferous in implied restriction and strictures to this natural development of personal style. It is rare indeed to find an illustration student who, at the outset, considers himself as a versatile image maker capable of handling diagrammatic work with creative and aesthetic insight as well as having a developed style for more personalised expressive problems. This current educational problem, not entirely confined to confirmed illustration students, affects, in varying degrees, many graphic design attitudes and constitutes a major problem in graphic educational policy. The required shift of emphasis to accommodate a wider spectrum of visual communication to embrace a virtually ignored area of technical

[3] U.S.A. equivalents: Grade 13 High School Pass = 'O' level
                       Lower division of 1st year University course = 'A' level

graphics, forms one of the objectives of the graphic design course under discussion.

Student reaction to both the experimental joint course and the more traditional illustration course proved both positive and confirming of educational design policy. Indeed, it has been found that the joint course, which begins with staff zeal and interest, inevitably ends with student interest and a work level intensity that virtually places all the staff on the rack! Which, of course, is just as it should be.

Because of the intentional inexactitude of student direction, a small number of students cross freely either way, between the illustration and first year design course, whilst one or two elect to leave the graphic design course entirely, the drop-out factor being well under the norm for a further education course; nonetheless, one feels that this decision is best reached earlier than later. The choice of a career for life is a very important matter.

Illustration for a sectional menu card for a proposed series in a presentation box. Third Year Diploma Course.

CHAPTER 7.

Occasionally colleges of art and design are called upon to provide some small social service for their immediate communities and for many years the graphic design department we have been discussing had, as an extra-mural activity, carried a share of this essentially worthwhile work. A request from the Intensive Care Unit of the Children's Burns Ward of a local hospital called for some pictures or murals for small children who, being severely burned, often spent several months upon their backs looking at a blank ceiling.

The second-year study programme, which included the integration of illustrators and designers on certain joint projects, were given the hospital request and asked to consider it as a design problem. Using design methodology, staff and students visited the Burns Ward and carried out information-gathering procedures which revealed not one problem but many that were varied and diverse, any one of which constituted a unique design situation. Apart from the children in the Intensive Care Unit there were very many categories of patient-based needs involving children of varying age groups in several stages of recuperation, from small bedridden infants to older children who might be walking patients undergoing degrees of plastic surgery.

In retrospect, the hospital project would seem to have fitted the nature of the course with uncanny exactness. The desirability of finding and using unique design situations which had no traditional solution, together with essential aspects of versatility and the development of socially adaptive attitudes was certainly part of the many objectives. However, the graphics course was, at that time, maturing its 'first' second year and whilst the reader may have been led to believe that the whole three-year course was a highly organised minutely time-tabled operation, in fact the ground ahead was virtually still unexplored Time was short and students, with over one third of their course completed, had very little in the way of traditional graphics to exhibit.

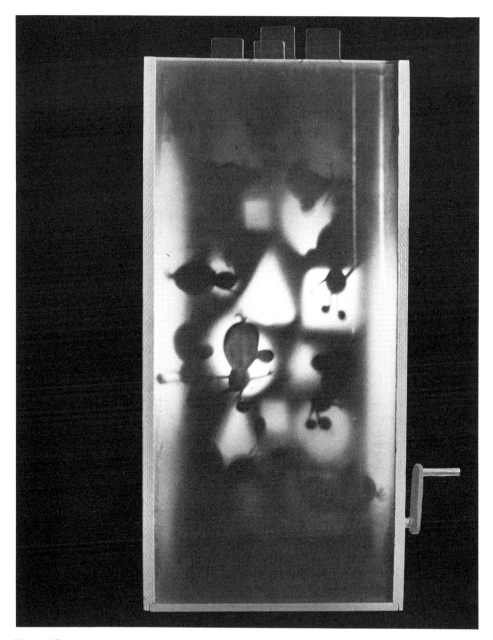

Hospital Burns Unit Project. Pictures both objective and abstract are projected
by back lighting and via a hand-operated moving belt on to a transparent textured
panel. A magazine of five alternatives is provided.
Note. The abstract images like the one depicted proved the most successful.

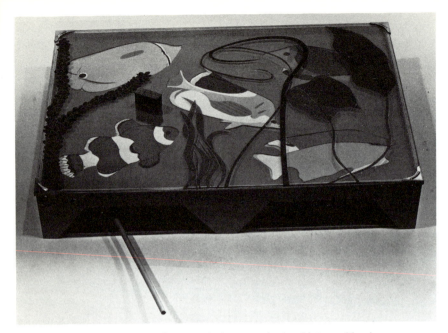

Magnetic jigsaw. Fish made up from metal pieces manipulated into position by a magnet. The idea evolved from the problems of a bedridden child with one hand bandaged trying to do a conventional jigsaw. *Below:* strip from BBC film.

A ground swell of concern was emanating from high places. Like ancestral voices prophesying war, the murmurs seem to ask "What are you about, graphics or antics?" *More importantly,* however, within the department serious revaluation and reconsideration was being given to the length of time the joint course had used and to the deductions made from the 'rank order of importance' of the basic graphic skill requirements: questions of expertise, of print technology, of creative imagery, of lettering of . . . the doubts were, at the time, real and valid. We simply could not ascertain, particularly from past traditional methods of 'teaching graphics' whether the students could cover the remaining ground. Consequently it very much appeared that time set aside for integrated illustrator and designer projects just would not allow much more then a brushing acquaintance with the hospital problem. We had, however, seen and heard the suffering children and that was impossible to dismiss as a mere academic curriculum consideration. We found ourselves honour-bound to do something, even if only as a token of good faith, perhaps even a pilot scheme to lay the way open for more extensive action when the course was less troubled by unknown factors and possibly more established as a valid diploma course.

With limited resources, the only finance available being the monies allocated to limited internal project work, and severe limitations regarding time and workshop facilities, we launched a pilot project. In the event, the work took much longer than anticipated; so long in fact that the telescoping pressures of the curriculum overtook it and for several months work was postponed. However, with the enthusiasm always to be associated with 'live' projects and the material assistance of workshop facilities and technical know-how from the now strongly forged links with the Construction Department, the pilot work was completed. The following twelve items may give an idea of the nature and range of the work involved:

Decorative textiles for bedscreens	Based on drawings made by the children of the Burns Unit. Silk screen printed.
Diversionary manipulative kinetic toy	A variable image kaleidoscope. Variety of motifs clipped to end of tube, lens rotated to give unlimited images.
Diversionary kinetic device	Motorised patterns making unit, giving a 30 minute cycle of changing patterns.
Diversionary manipulative kinetic device	For use by children with at least one free hand.
Diversionary, manipulative and kinetic	Picture Box. Pictures — both objective and abstract are projected by back lighting and via a moving belt (hand driven) on to a textured panel. A magazine of five alternatives are provided.
Diversional	Suspended animal mobile. Polystyrene and coloured paper.
Diversional	Woollen panda. Tactile image attractive to children, but ward hygiene dictated the placing behind a perspex panel.
Diversional, manipulative	Glass marble machine toy. Marble activated vertical conveyor.
Diversional	Hot air activated mobile.
Diversional	Magnetic jigsaw. Fish made up from metal pieces and manipulated into position from above and below by a magnet. Note: perspex covered with applied ornament of pond weed.
Diversional, educational	Mobile. National costumes and flags. Abstract.
Diversional	Print material for perspex faced panels wall or ceiling fixing.

The project made no pretence of being anything other than an excursion into an uncharted area of visual communication; much was learned by the students regarding suitability of purpose and the limitations of economy, time and, in this particular instance, an additional discipline of extreme hygiene. The four ceilings which comprised the intensive care unit created the severest hygiene problems and consequently the surgeons and ward sisters advised against any device that might harbour the slightest speck of dust, the result being that the 'mobiles' planned for the units, which were in fact glass walled cells, were hung outside where they were easily visible through the glass partitions. Although a system of projected images proved the only practical solution to the ceiling problems, it could not be employed due to financial limitations; however, three years later a charity organisation has promised assistance to this aspect of the graphic design department's activities and it is hoped that a solution to the initial request, made three years ago, may yet be realised.

Why did we not paint a mural and have done with it? The answer may be best explained by the reasoning behind the picture-box project — that any static pictorial matter must become boring after six hours, positively irritating after twelve; consequently we felt unable to produce a picture that would hold up after a possible full six-month continuous scrutiny.

The project proved so valuable in so many different ways that it became, despite its time-consuming nature, a feature in the second year combined illustrator/designer projects. In the following second-year studies, when a more stable position was reached regarding timetable pressures, a brief was prepared for the students, who were required to produce visual aids for the use of the staff and pupils of a school for the deaf. The following brief and programme is possibly self-explanatory.

1.0 Educational Visual Aids for Instructing Deaf Children.

2.0 This school for the deaf is a special school catering for age groups ranging from $2\frac{1}{2}$ years to 16 years. The school consists of seven main groups divided according to age and ability.

3.0 It is proposed that teams of two students will work with each group to study some of the problems faced by the teacher and in consultation with the group teacher, tackle a particular problem relevant to the group to which the team is attached. Study proposals leading to prototype schemes that can be tested by the staff and children are aimed for.

4.0 As language learning is the key to all the other subjects, particular emphasis is put on it because of the difficulty that a deaf child has in understanding and practising it.

Staff and student discussing the counting game project, a pictorial plotting game being an extension of the Cuisinaire system.

5.0 In conventional methods of teaching language to deaf children, the concept of sign/object relationship must be grasped first of all, before vocabulary of word/object relationships can be extended. Sign-object relationship can be indicated by lip gesture, sound magnification, body gesture, pictorial signs, etc.

6.0 Programme.

6.1 Monday October 14th 3.00 p.m. Studio
Discussion on the problems involved and background information with the headmaster, deputy head and members of staff.

6.2 Wednesday October 16th 9.30 a.m. Studio
Visit to the school for instruction, investigation and appraisal of the problem.

6.3 Wednesday October 16th 1.30 p.m. Studio.
Compile situation report for further discussion.

6.4 Thursday 17th October.
Individual projects according to discussion with group teacher.
Timetable according to individual requirements.

7.0 Friday 8th November 1.30 p.m. Studio.
Project assessment and evaluation.

8.0 The following points must be considered when designing your proto-types:

8.1 Production economy. It is most likely that, if successful your ideas will be made by teaching staff with minimum equipment and money.
Materials should be selected and ideas followed with this in mind.

8.2 Versatility – a design with this attribute should enable it to be used in a number of teaching situations other than the specific one you had in mind.

8.3 Simplicity should be aimed for in components and construction and also to enable immediate use.

8.4 Your solution must be well within the concept of the age group you are working with and should also be related to previous and future years' activities. Investigate this point as it is important that you do not overlap unnecessarily.

Student solutions were practical, diverse and imaginative. One of the most successful, a book with split pages for teaching the tenses of verbs for the 11–15 age group equally involved the talents of an illustrator and a designer. The following student report gives essentials of the project:

Book showing pictorial illustrations of the past, present and future tenses of the verb, with appropriate colour code.

A device enabling the simple re-arrangement of sentence structure by rotating and replacing various drums.

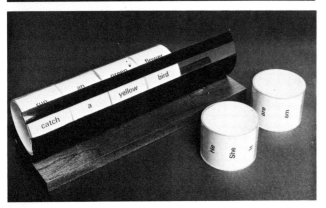

1. Problem emerged after discussion that the children have difficulty in understanding tenses and it was on this aspect that an attempt was made to help.

2. The vehicle for instruction was to be a book backed by a set of story boards which repeated the content of the book and were to be used by the teacher as demonstration aids.

2.2 Two basic reasons for the choice of a "book" vehicle.

2.3 This type of vehicle was in general use in the upper half of the school.

2.4 The senior forms would use the information for reference.

2.5 The junior classes would use the book as a means of instruction.

3. The information in the book to be of two types, typographic and illustrated. Both "means" conveying the same message.

4. Three items of each verb to be shown on each page.

4.1 The first depicts future tense, the second present, the third past.

4.2 The illustration and typographic information would represent each tense of the same verb.

4.3 The third person singular was to be used in all tenses in both written and illustrative information.

5. The reason for placing the tenses in the order of future, present, past:

5.1 To explain either the future or the past of any given action to another person, one must talk about the action. For this reason the illustration describing the present is placed in the centre.

5.2 Before a person carries out the action he must first have thought about it to some degree in depth. Whether it is a fraction of a second or an hour, he predicts a course of action in the future, therefore placing the future tense first in the scheme, present second, past last.

6. A vertical type of binding was decided on as the easiest to operate. A loose leaf binding is necessary so that the illustrations and text can be separated.

6.1 The book was to be A4 paper size, printed silkscreen on PVC.

7. Some verbs to be illustrated / irregular verbs – drive, eat, drink, make, hit, catch, write, read, ride, throw, run, sit stand; regular – push, pull, mend, kick, hammer, jump, walk.

7.1 The children have already learned the meaning of the above regular verbs.

8. Colour code – green for the future, red for the past, blue for the present. This code ties in with method used by teacher at the school.

Many projects involved three-dimensional problem-solving in the form of games to teach these deaf children to relate word and objects (nouns), to count — including the use of fractions and decimals, or simply to learn a number of words. Using game theory to give a sense of involvement, colour codes and attractive devices, the projects included

a shake — or chance — word selection game backed up by a card index of images;

an extension of the Cuisinaire system using a set of counting sticks with dot numeration combined with a pictorial plotting game;

a geometrical proportion or fraction teaching aid in cut-out shapes to reinforce through the handling of shapes;

two split-page books giving body movements and facial expressions, with associated terminology;

a tiddley-winks game with a conversion to decimal scoring system.

Apart from its many-sided values, the project for the school for the deaf imposed certain necessary constraints on the personal styles of students in the illustration group. To acknowledge the specific audience for their work these students were made aware that personal decorative treatment should not detract from statements of fact. Thus the tree illustration that was confused with a flower and the tail of a fish being too similar to that of a bird required adjustments that made the illustrator more aware of the functional nature of his imagery.

The research area uncovered by the deaf school project proved as exciting as it was frustrating. We simply did not know the boundaries of the fundamental problems and mysteries inherent in human communication and desperately required the assistance of someone who was more fully knowledgeable in the subject. Staff and students involved were loath to leave the project and although other duties beckoned, it was vowed to return to the subject in the following year when information and experience gained, together with staff research, might possibly produce one more step towards applying graphics with more understanding and validity.

In the interests of continuity, it is necessary that we return to the events following the Burns Unit project and other projects of the second-year studies. The hospital complex provided excellent material for a theoretical signing exercise for second-year graphic design students whilst the Construction Department also carried out an extensive analysis of the architectural problems involved in the Burns Unit organisation. Two large, open-air playground toys, a pedal operated boat and a steam engine were also produced by the students of the Construction Department and partly fulfilled a much needed feature for this outdoor facility.

Subsequent to the hospital project, the second-year graphics programme concerned itself more closely with basic skills and problems requiring print solutions which inevitably involved cross reference across all the basic skills and projects of the course.

Based on the simple use of the camera and photographic materials as a recording tool in the first-year studies, the approach to photography was widened to consider its application as a graphic design subject. For the purposes of applying photography to any problem, it was considered as consisting of five divisions; subject, lighting, optics, film and printing method, students being encouraged to analyse their problems and solutions relative to these elements. The following projects indicate the more formal instruction in photography; other experience, less mechanical in nature, came from the use of photography in many aspects of other second-year project work.

Problem: produce a rectangular container for a chosen object with photographic representation of the object on all six faces. This problem of precise scale and geometrically correct representation of a given subject, such as a torch, apple, screw-driver, etc., involved the use of artificial lighting and various studio techniques to allow the object to be isolated from any background.

Problem: make a wall chart, to a given dimension, to explain photo-graphically the assembly or function of an object such as an Anglepoise lamp, mincing machine, etc. The solution to this exercise could involve multiple exposures in the camera, multi-printings of registered negatives — each having appropriate values of sharp, smear and so on, depending on the effect required, thus giving the students experience in pre-visualising, proportional exposures of a moving object with appropriate lighting and accurate hand registration.

More open-ended projects, which involved both the illustration and the design students, required the production of a photographic essay concerned with any aspect about children and the production of a poster to a given size, to include and convey the meaning of a certain word such as psycho, fear, collector, danger, with an image clear enough to convey the meaning. The project produced much experience in the optical considerations of placing one word relative to the image.

Formal instruction in the use of the ciné camera as a graphic tool and various cinematic uses such as animation techniques concluded the set

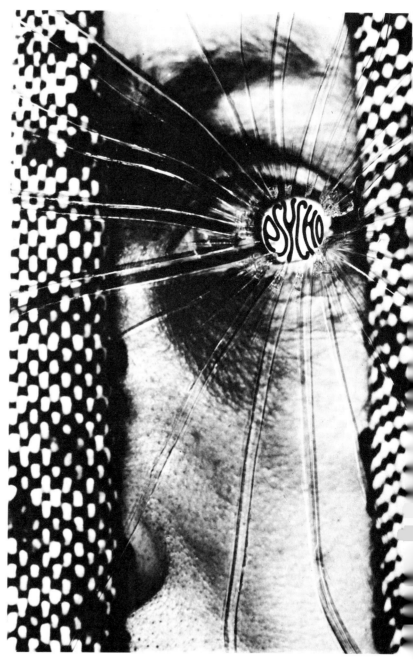

Photographic project; the placing of one word to an image while developing
photographic techniques, the image conveying the meaning of the word.

instruction in photography. Basically the projects and photographic investigations required the student to understand fully the various cinematic processes and techniques in order to be able to specify precise instructions and to gain some versatility in the medium. For those students who wished to specialise in the photographic and cinematic media, the course formed a base for their third year studies. Technical illustration, which had reached a point of optimum experience necessary for the general purposes of a graphic designer, realised a three-dimensional design project of an interlocking carriage or tray device, consisting of containers (cups) which locked together to facilitate the transportation of liquid in such conditions as a moving railway carriage, ship, etc. With varying degrees of success, each student produced three-dimensional mock-ups of their devices. They also produced associated sales and descriptive leaflets, etc.

Projects using existing material concerning the National Parks and Forestry undertakings were deliberately scrambled, thus requiring the student to employ copy analysis techniques such as flow charts, rank orders, etc., before specifying and producing a typographical printed specimen.

A complete house style for an imaginary boutique not only required all the associated typography of letterheads, envelopes, swing tickets and invoices, but also the styling of the shop front itself.

The signs for the controls of a switchboard panel of a certain electronic device involved the potential user in a 'learned programme' situation. The signs for these controls, therefore, became apt vehicles for further development of semiotic[1] theory. This signing project was preceded by a series of special lectures on semiotics in addition to data from an electronics engineer.

It will have been noted that the basic skills involved cross reference across all the projects of the course, acting as vehicles of versatility with which students were able to solve problems with increasing fluency. At all times functional aspects were stressed, with aesthetics left to the students' own personal intuitive levels. It would be tedious to the reader to list every single project of these second year studies which in every case, to a greater or lesser degree, involved the design process and print technology. Perhaps a mention should be made of results obtained from a period set aside for the students to produce an individual silkscreen printed image which omitted words and defined a personal message considered important to our time and age. The results

[1] Theory of signs and symbols.

Control panel for electronic switchgear. Practical approach to semiotic theory.

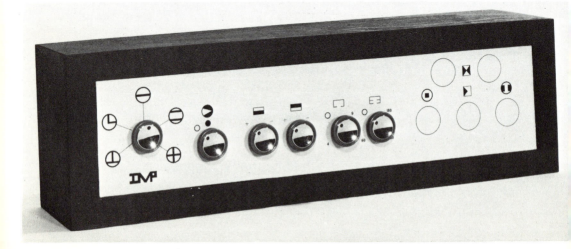

were startling and informative; a quiet, retiring female student produced incredibly powerful references to illegal abortion, whilst another sharply focussed a naked Prime Minister as a cherub, astride a Renaissance fountain tortoise (forgetting perhaps that the tortoise eventually won the race!) Other works concerned immigration, population explosion, waste-making societies, war, and so on. On show for weekly criticism and debate, the combined work presented such a galaxy of powerful, evocative and uninhibited visual statements that had one of the more conservative visitors strayed into the studio, it is certain that strong reservations to the Governors would have been made in respect of departmental policy!

Specific illustration projects, giving expression to individual student's development of pictorial image-making also concerned information gathering, sorting and problem-solving techniques. A project perhaps representative of course philosophy called upon the student to produce two illustrations for two historical, sociological incidents for a theoretical series of articles for a Sunday newspaper. Each called upon the students to research and synthesise the complex subject matter of the abdication of King Edward VIII and the associated factors of Government, Church and public opinion, together with the interaction and events of the Shostakovitch and Stalin incidents[2]. Students were asked to check the facts and prepare the graphic presentation in black and white for line block reproduction on newsprint. This elementary skill, from previous experience, we found to have been a much neglected feature in the illustrator's repertoire.

A different project, drawing more directly on categorisation and ordering, concerned a pictorial presentation of certain statistical information regarding the local city; facts such as unemployment, accommodation, comparative income and spending according to geographical and sociological factors. Use of city amenities — swimming baths, libraries, public transport, etc., were to be portrayed in a simple symbolised manner in the form of a printed broadsheet.

Towards the end of the academic year the preparation of a photo-lithographic printed package was initiated in readiness for production immediately after the summer vacation. Involving three-dimensional geometry, the preliminary academic content concerned five exercises in which the investigation of ratio and proportion, arithmetic, geometric, harmonic, logarithmic and the Fibonacci ratios, followed by a practical

[2] During the Stalinist regime the composer Shostakovitch earned the disfavour of the Soviet Government by writing allegedly bourgeois music.

exercise in the form of space organisation. Using cocktail sticks, balsa cement, paper, board and elastic bands, students constructed the space frames known as the platonic solids, i.e. cube, tetrahedron, octahedron, dodecahedron and nosahedron. The development of this in the next exercise explored the mathematical permutations and multi-locking properties of these elements, together with other prisms such as the triagonal and hexagonal. The final exercise explored the interrelation of forms as inserts, cushioning product supports and various stability formulae. This background research for packaging structures was not intended to pre-determine results but to serve as a basis of knowledge of three-dimensional form. With reference to certain photo-lithographic procedures and limitations particular to the department's print workshop, they constituted a base from which a point-of-sale package design was required. The brief asked for a dual purpose non-disposable pack, firstly to contain a bathroom toilet commodity and, secondly, to form a series of children's interlocking educational toys. The completion of the package project early in the following term concluded the formal based studies and as a development from broad based activities of the second year, third-year studies were constructed from a careful appraisal of individual student preference, development and potentials, requiring specialist tutors who either embraced combinations of, or specific interests in typography, photography, exhibition design, ciné film and television design or illustration.

For certain students some specialisation had occurred at the end of the previous term, concerned with two extra-mural activities which were considered to contain values acceptable to the general course direction.

The extra-mural activities, which commenced in the second year but continued into the third, consisted of graphics for two films produced by an educational film unit attached to a neighbouring university of technology and a direct commission from the Forestry Commission in respect of a mobile exhibition unit. The films concerned the physics of the ionisation of gases in relation to geiger counters and read-out equipment of cathode ray tubes, etc., and an educational survey of certain social aspects of secondary school education. In each case the students involved carried out these design activities separately to their normal second-year course work, the only course time involved being two or three days to attend initial conferences with directors and film technicians in order to be fully aware of policies, technicalities

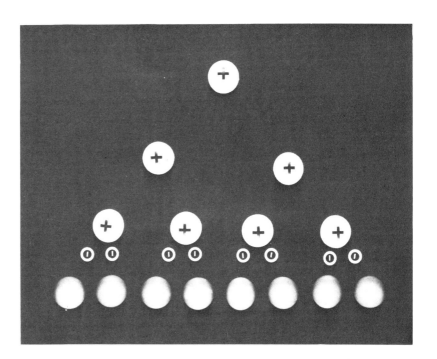

Stills from animated film for a
neighbouring university.
Subject: The working of a
Geiger counter.

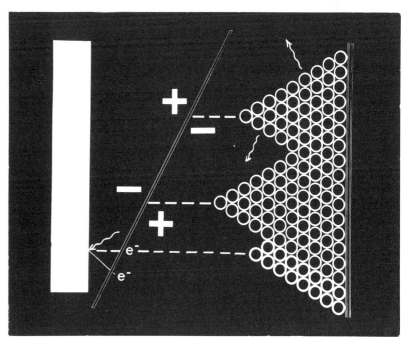

and purpose of graphic requirements. In the event, the students, apart from producing the graphics which involved animation techniques, also carried out a considerable amount of the actual film production.

Exhibition design, like package design, forms a synthesis of two- and three-dimensional design. The Forestry Commission, or more correctly, the Horticultural Society affiliated to the Commission exhibition project, provided an ideal justification of course concepts and may therefore be described in some detail.

The production of a moveable, free-standing display of graphics, horticultural specimens and printed literature, had the initial purpose of informing schools, district councils and the general public of the aims of the Society, these being to stimulate the care of trees and the appreciation of their beauty and to establish the necessity of main-taining a balanced natural environment.

It was realised that the display could point to a very wide field, including tree identification, propagation, preservation, produce, use of timber, environmental importance — not only functional but also historical and aesthetic. The information gathering and sorting alone took several months of the student's spare time, providing an ideal example of the functional properties of the 'design process'. The final categorisation produced the following emphasis in subject matter:

What are trees? — definition, structure, identification and seasonal changes.

Man's need of trees — without them we die (nitrogen absorption, erosion drainage, noise reduction, etc.)

The beauty of trees: aesthetic (landscape, building, towns and cities . . . random clearance for motor cars and habitation).

The care of trees: Vandalism, bad pruning, bad organisation. If we are to keep trees we must understand them.

Produce of trees: Fruits, foliage, rubber, amber, resin, ashes, timber, etc.

Trees and life: Tree as habitat for birds, insects, squirrels, etc.

Symbolism and Myths: The Tree of Life (Ygdrasil) Tree of Good and Evil (Adam and Eve), sacred groves (Druids), Tree of Wisdom (Celtic), Tree of Peace (olive), Tree of Fertility (Hawthorn) and so on.

Relative to the financial budget, the student designer evolved, with assistance from the Construction Department, a system of two-sided display panels (perspex sheets with graphics in between) and a simple peg device for easy assembly. Shelves, for objects and printed speci-mens, utilised a simple 'hook on' technique. In 4ft sections the graphics

Official Programme

International Congress
Home Economics **68** Bristol

Congress Theme

Home Economics in the Service of
International Co-operation

21 - 27 July 1968

University of Bristol, England

Thursday 25 July

**XI
68**

Association of Home Economics of Great Britain

Congress Reception
Reception at the Grand Spa, Clifton, Bristol

Thursday 25 July

**XI
68**

The Further Education Staff College

Congress Reception
Buffet Supper at Combe Lodge, Blagdon

Departing at   **hours**
from your **Hall of Residence**
Coach P

Manor Hall

Rodney Lodge

XI
68

Symphony Concert by the **Bournemouth Symphony Orchestra**
conductor **Constantin Sylvestri**

XI International Congress
Home Economics **68** Bristol

Admission by this Programme

in the Colston Hall, Bristol
(Entertainments Manager F.K.Cowley MIM Ent)

Hostess Association

**United Kingdom Federation for
Education in Home Economics**

Typography for a conference.

paid attention to the placing of reading material, giving essentials at average eye level and other information at various appropriate points, care being also taken not to give too much text at any given point due to the limitations of reading ability in the standing position.

Utilising a four-column grid, the reading distance of diagrams, text and photographs were amongst the other factors used by the student designer.

Apart from the obvious educational advantages to the student, being thus employed in real design, wide benefits also accrued to the course as a functional organism in society. This fact had been more than confirmed in the previous third year when a student became involved with the organisation and graphics for an international conference of Home Economics which, being held for the first time in Great Britain and outside a capital city, provided a great challenge to the general concepts of this graphic course. The lessons provided by this project were to prove of much importance and consequence to the course. At the first meeting, called in response to a request for graphic assistance by the chief organiser of the conference, some surprise was shown by the conference organisers that our interest lay beyond 'designing the front cover of the conference programme'. They were more amazed at the suggestion that a student should produce all the graphics of the conference as a single, unified, design project. The events revealed that most of the organisational details concerned with welcoming, transporting and distributing two thousand foreign-speaking delegates in and around our city, with booking arrangements for concerts, halls of residence, sub-committees, etc., had yet to be finalised. Since most of the informative graphics clearly should be produced and forwarded to the delegates before arrival, it was obvious that, allowing for estimating costs and printing time, the student-designer would be immediately plunged into considerable organisational methodology. A student less confident in systematic design and organisation capacity would most probably have retired at this point. To her credit, however, the student-designer covered every aspect of the graphic requirements made by the two-week conference, including a last minute translation of a section of the programme from English to French and taking full responsibility for financial estimate, budget control (which meant the selection of an appropriate printer), invoicing and proof reading.

The third-year studies produced a pattern of diverse interest. A designer and one illustrator elected to concentrate on ciné film and closed-

Newcomen's Atmospheric Pumping Engine, 1712

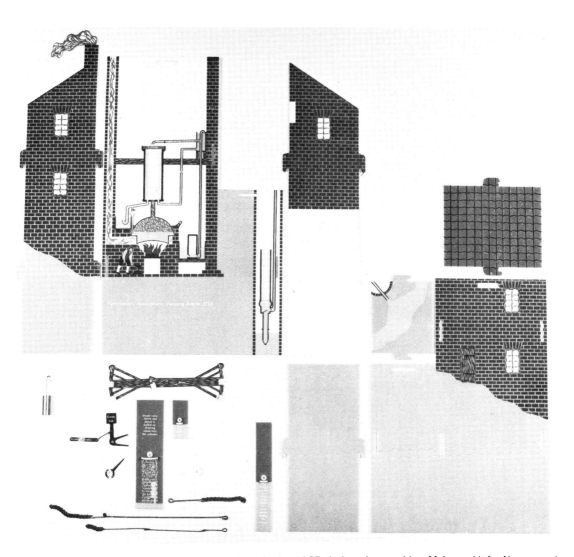

3rd Year Project. Option of 3D design plus graphics. Make-up kit for Newcomen's Atmospheric Pumping Engine. Student investigated learning processes of young people and concluded that the manipulation of pieces to construct a "beam engine" was more viable than tracing a diagram in a book.
Illustrations show above, unassembled pieces and opposite, front and rear view of assembled unit.

Circuit Set Unit. Continuous stationery project.
Unit on typewriter, side view
Unit on typewriter, front view

circuit television techniques, producing by means of animated drawing, an account of the slave trade; an imaginative children's story of a tiger; and a film of experimental imagery using film process techniques to produce a coloured moiré effect. (In subsequent years, students wishing to specialise in this media undertake a set programme in conjunction with the General Studies Department producing closed-circuit television visual aids for various primary schools in the area, in each case the student being required to use problem-solving techniques for the specific subject set.) Three students, not wishing to specialise, decided to follow a general graphic programme with an emphasis on educational visual aids, one returning to the 'Burns' hospital to carry out an indoor educational playground project to the special requirements of a play area set aside in one of the wards.

Other student directions included exhibition design – producing an informative display panel (of the structure of cells for use in schools or the nursing profession) and an educational aid consisting of a free standing unit, from which small children could detach sequential elements to provide information on any given subject. An illustration student completely redesigned the format of an information manual of the Department of Veterinary Studies at the local university, and apart from re-categorising the material, furnished it with on-the-spot drawings of animals undergoing tests, of operations, of apparatus and diagrams.

Most students attended an optional lecture programme concerning aspects of professional practice from the director of a leading practising agency or design group. More formal lectures provided by the Faculty of Business and Professional Studies constituted: Marketing, i.e.

concept of marketing, product planning, distribution including resale price maintenance, consumer behaviour, sales promotion, sales organisation, market research, survey of planning, consumer protection, sales forecasting, export marketing and industrial marketing; also economics, statutory laws, psychology and the code of advertising practice, together with administration and media.

Most problems involved design methodology in varying degrees of depth and all work was directed to a printed end-product. Possibly the most interesting results developed from what was originally considered as a one-week project, that is to say, a stop-gap operation between two major projects, which required the students to re-assess the purpose of a number of items, which included bus and railway

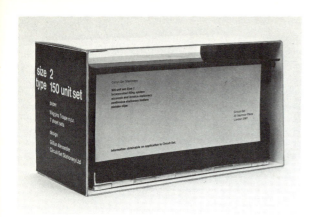

The packaging of the Circuit Set

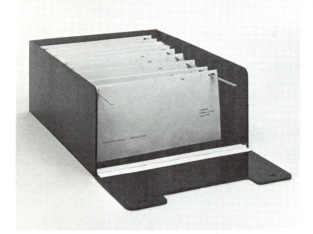

System of filing (to a normal filing cabinet)

Circuit Set separate from typewriter

Circuit-Set is a system of continuous stationery for use in conjunction with a typewriter. It is designed to adjust to any office system and work in conjunction with systems already established, using Circuit-Set invoicing and filing to complete the unit efficiency. The unit which encloses the paper is designed to feed it through the typewriter, to collect and refold the resulting pile in a tray at the back. There are no moving parts to this unit, it is powered only by the paperflow movements of the typewriter.

Circuit-Set
20 Seymour Place
London SW7

Circuit-Set Stationery

The paper is folded and held in a stack which, if held horizontally, forms a narrow and compact filing system.

The paper is fitted into the unit by a downward pressure of the thumbs into the rubber-sided case (a) whose resistance prevents the paper from falling back and holds it rigid while in use.

Circuit-Set
20 Seymour Place
London SW7

Circuit-Set Stationery

The unit is then fixed onto the typewriter with the attachments provided (or available on application to Circuit-Set and statement of typewriter make and model.)

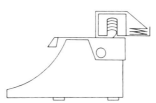

Circuit-Set
20 Seymour Place
London SW7

Circuit-Set Stationery

**300 unit set Size 1
incorporated filing system
accounts and invoice stationery
continuous stationery leaflets
mistake slips**

Circuit-Set
20 Seymour Place
London SW7

Information obtainable on application to Circuit-Set.

timetables, stationery, publicity, filing systems, maps and catalogues. Students produced interesting revaluations of these perennial problems, such as a complete route map for the Corporation omnibus company – allowing a visitor to find his way to any part of the city without verbal directions – and a plastic, fan-opening, pocket-sized train timetable. One student produced a very clear assessment of a possible requirement for certain large companies or commercial organisations in respect of continuous stationery in relation to their present stationery and filing systems. Having thus established the validity of her problem, the student proceeded to invent and manufacture a device or unit, later patented under the copyright title of 'Circuit-Set', for use in conjunction with a typewriter. In the student's own words, it is designed to adjust to any office system and work in conjunction with systems already established, using Circuit-Set invoicing and filing to complete the unit efficiency. The unit which encloses the paper is designed to feed it through the typewriter, to collect and refold the resulting pile in a tray at the back. There are no moving parts to this unit; it is powered only by the paper flow movements of the type-writer. The system for filing continuous stationery consisted of a simple method of suspension from two parallel bars within a normal filing cabinet drawer system. In an office containing many typists the economic savings in time, labour and money made the Circuit-Set system a very viable proposition. Although aware of computer-continuous-stationery techniques, it should be recorded that similar industrial investigations into the same problem concerning typewriters and filing systems were entirely unknown to the student at the time of the research and development. Subsequently, the Circuit-Set has proved superior to all other proposed solutions.

The dramatic aspect of this student project lies in its early proof of the validity of one of the objectives of the experimental design course – that of versatility. Because of first-year design projects and experience and education in design methodology, together with the recovering of certain lost values inherent in technical drawing and three-dimensional design techniques, the student possessed freedom to move across a whole section of the design spectrum from graphics to product design and, in the final analysis, to an aspect of business management. It is the nature of some problems to escalate beyond the confines originally conceived as possibly framing the solution. The 'one-week project' that initiated the Circuit-Set developed into the student's major project for diploma assessment and, in its final presentation, included all associated graphics such as informative and descriptive leaflets, advertising and packaging.

Students following the more generalised aspect of graphic design were given several projects as optional extras to their individual enquiries. The outline of three projects may assist in showing the general direction of this aspect of third-year studies.

The first concerned an enquiry into motivations inherent in the practice of using coporate images, the brief reading thus:

The present preoccupation in commerce of 'establishing an image' in order to create instant identification and thereby increase sales has produced a priority where motives have become blurred by the over-whelming supply of visual projections. This project is concerned with examination of these motives, a re-definition of objectives and an investigation into their effects.

1. Prepare a definitive statement on what a corporate identity is, and, by examples, establish whether it is a natural or unnatural phenomenon.

2. List and examine the causes which have produced the need for identity as between individuals and as between the individual and the group.

3. Take one situation and its related causes and define the objectives of its instigator/s.

4. Within the same situation, establish the effects both on the individual and the group. Remember that the individual can be projecting an image to the group (society).

5. Prepare your conclusions and state your opinions of the validity of a corporate identity — re-defining item 1. if necessary.

6. From all the copy and material produced, prepare a presen-tation, the form of which to be suggested by the content, i.e. do not attempt pre-conceptions until items 1. to 5. have been established.

One student took the situation of the Salvation Army, whilst another undertook a preliminary investigation into the need of a corporate image for the newly constituted Polytechnic, of which the graphic design department itself formed a constituent part. Upon the basis of this work a further brief was evolved to give the student, whose specialised interest lay in typography, actual experience of examining this highly complex problem as a major project, the briefing being as follows:

1. You are required to produce proposals for a corporate identity and its implementation for the proposed Polytechnic. Work involved will be broadly as follows:
2. Collection and analysis of all printed matter used at present by the constituent colleges.
3. Policy meeting with the Polytechnic Director and/or other responsible person, at which meeting the results of 2 will be presented.
The further purpose of the meeting will be to determine:
'tone' or 'style' of the Polytechnic
sharing of facilities/printing/computer
rationalisation of printed matter (e.g. whether 1 or 3 prospectuses etc.)
4. Presentation of design proposals based on a thorough under-standing of 2 and 3. This will concern decisions regarding formats and image of printed matter but may also include signing etc.
Suggestions for analysis —
Collect all printed matter
used internally and externally
printed internally and externally
Produce checklist to find:
Omissions
over-lap of material (where there is an over-lap does one solution work better than others?)
Classify:
under general headings;
to indicate source of printer (internal or external);
according to size (for subsequent rationalisation suggestions).

The second project concerned an informative persuasive campaign for the prevention of fire in the home. The brief was for a small portable freestanding display capable of use on window shelves, tables and desks etc. (portability being interpreted as facilitating dismantling to packaged form to dimensions permitting easy carrying by hand, fitting the passenger seat of a car and through the post). Primary data regarding the ten major causes of home fires were included in the brief but students were required to assess and use their own copy in conjunction with such pictorial matter as their solutions demanded. The investigation into the techniques of persuasive psychology constitutes the third example of third-year projects. Students were required to produce two full-sized posters to show the opposing ideas of anti-smoking and tobacco promotion; of famine and food promotion; religious beliefs and certain opposing society factors, etc. As with the fire prevention project, all visual material, copywriting and process reproduction preparation had to be the student's own creative work. In contrast to this methodology approach, other third-year projects consisted of exercises in re-styling of problems already solved. The results of this conscious and deliberate attention to these forms of creativity more than confirmed the initial suspicion that the prominence these elements had held in previous graphic design education had been very much over-stressed. It would seem, from our observations, that students are either fully alive to the climate of fashion or maintain a deficiency that no education can eradicate. Abilities in aesthetic judgement and pictorial expressiveness largely belong to the intuitive processes and consequently it was interesting to observe the individual student's ability to define the functional, clinical root of a solution to a problem and then to consider and apply the essential additional element of functional styling.

It should be re-stated that at all times throughout the course students were free to test their intuitive processes against design methodology and, in the case of illustration students, this proved to be quite a common event! As previously indicated, these students, using a high degree of aesthetic, subjective pictorial matter, could not be expected fully to analyse their creative styles in so formal and detached a manner; however, in many instances such as in the deaf school project, the need to produce illustrations for a specific audience gave the student some appreciation of the wider terms of reference to their personal form of expression.

CONCLUSIONS

This diploma course proposes a framework from which all graphic activities may be understood. A generalised strategy such as this, however, must raise many issues about specialisation and specific vocational training. This dilemma of binary education plagues all aspects of further education. For graphics it seemed to bring into focus not only the specialisations of typography, photography and technical illustration, but also the whole question of producing 'stylists' who may be asked to work in design teams dealing with all types of commercial design work. The issue is further complicated by the historical emphasis of the importance of the intuitive and artistic processes in this activity. The balance between all these elements varies from one course to another but in our experience overdue emphasise on fine art and the intuitive processes had caused an over-preoccupation with styles and aesthetic appearance. On the other hand, the logics inherent in typography had produced a greater degree of overall appreciation of the act of 'designing'. The platitude 'specialisation leads to fossilisation' was not, we found, entirely true. Since, like certain aspects of natural history which reveal that some species not only survive because of their specialised features but lead to further evolutionary forms because of these features, typography provided a widening factor, whilst our misuse of fine art had caused an anaesthetic torpor. The diploma course I have described sought the essential balance between all these factors by the means stated.

Indications of a wider industrial application of graphic design — that is, separate from traditional usages and employment in advertising and publishing — are beginning to materialise in employment notices and advertisements. Specialist visual communicators are required for Town and Country Planning, Highway Committees and architects' offices. The visual clamour caused by competing street advertising in our cities, towns and villages often saturates important informative and directional traffic signs, etc. Awakening to this problem, a gradual trickle of graphic design employment or recruitment to planning teams concerned with the functional operation, as well as concepts of a 'street picture', is rapidly becoming a common feature. Requests from architectural consultants, consortiums and practices for visual communication units, must herald a possible growing interest from all large industrial concerns since their directional, informative and warning signing systems are often confused whilst in some cases their internal stationery and other visual communication systems result from practices that have their origin in the pre-telephone era.

From primary to university education levels, graphic and audio aids are almost a daily feature and, indeed, many university departments are either employing graphic designers, or formulating service departments for this specific purpose. In the television media (which often requires an all-round knowledge of constructional design for use in animation techniques, set construction and layout, as well as the more generally known activities of persuasive advertising tricks and programme-credit illustrations and story-board techniques) graphic design contains the powerful potential of educational visual aids. Teaching or learning programme methods, which are at present a major American educational factor, cannot be far removed from a more important role in the European educational scene.

These signs and trends in internal social development, which constitute the tip of the iceberg, must indicate an increasing emphasis on the importance of the thought process in graphic design education. But what of intuition or creativity — how will these fare in a world that marshals knowledge, fact, methodology and function as amongst the first principles of design? History surely gives the answer to this in that no great invention or creative leap in art or science has occurred in complete and utter isolation. The route exists, sometimes in the individual's preliminary work, often in the spirit of the times and occasionally in a manner borrowed from earlier times. The work of Michelangelo and Leonardo da Vinci could not have occurred without the spirit and motivation of the Renaissance; Gutenberg could hardly have invented his adjustable type mould if he had not grown up in the technologically minded city of Mainz, and so on . . .

History, if it teaches anything about creativity, intuition and invention, surely indicates that 'fortune favours the prepared mind'. As educators our task is clear.

1. *A pictorial history of invention*   Umberto Eco & G. B. Zorzoli   Weidenfeld & Nicolson 1962
2. *The Great Russian Experiment-Russian Art*   Camilla Gray   Thames & Hudson 1962
3. *Printing and the Mind of Man*   British Museum 1963
4. *The Typographic Arts*   Stanley Morison   The Sylvan Press 1950
5. *Five hundred years of printing*   S. H. Steinberg   Penguin Books 1955
6. *Anatomy of Printing*   John Lewis   Faber and Faber 1970
7. *'50 Years Bauhaus' Exhibition*   Walter Gropius, Ludwig Grote etc.   Royal Academy of Arts 1968
8. *The Illustration of Books*   David Bland   Faber and Faber 1958
9. *What is a Designer: education and practice*   Norman Potter   Studio Vista 1969
10. *Pioneers of Modern Design*   Nikolaus Pevsner   Penguin Books 1960
11. *The Sources of Modern Architecture and Design*   Nikolaus Pevsner   Thames & Hudson 1968
12. *Basic Design: the dynamics of visual form*   Maurice de Sausmarez   Studio Vista
13. *William Morris as designer*   Ray Watkinson   Studio Vista 1967
14. *The Non-objective World*   Kasimir Malevich   Paul Theobold Company Chicago 1959
15. *The Story of Art*   E. H. Gomrich   Phaidon 1961
16. *The Human Use of Human Beings*   Norbert Wiener   Sphere Books 1968
17. *The Computer in Art*   Jasia Reichardt   Studio Vista 1971
18. *Typographica* – articles by Herbert Spencer and Camilla Grey, Ken Garland and Eckhard Neumann 1960–1968
19. *The New Vision*   Laszlo Moholy-Nagy   Wittenborn 1946
20. *Recall of Educational Cybernetics and applied linguistics*   M. J. Apter article Professor Helmar Frank   1969
21. *The Origins of Form in Art*   Herbert Read   Thames & Hudson 1965
22. *Grafilm: an approach to a new medium*   J. Bryn Daniel   Studio Vista 1970
23. *ULM Journal of the Ulm School for Design*   Various   1964–1968
24. *Computer Typesetting in the UK*   H. J. Davis
25. *Operational Research*   Eric Duckworth   Methuen 2nd ed. 1965
26. *The Art of the Soluble*   P. M. Medawar   Methuen 1967
27. *The Bauhaus*   Hans M. Wingler   MIT Press 1969
28. *Engineering Heritage Vol I*   D. J. Booker   Heinemann 1963
29. *Anatomy of Judgement*   M. L. J. Abercrombie   Hutchinson 1960
30. *The Book*   D. C. McMurtrie   Oxford University Press 1957
31. *Films as Art*   Rudolph Arnheim   Faber and Faber 1958
32. *Techniques of Advertising Photography*   Joachim Giehelhausen   Nickolaus Karpf 1963